BRIDGE OVER BRITAIN

BRIDGE OVER BRITAIN

THE BEST OF BRITISH REGIONAL FOOD

Tom Bridge

Photographs by David George

CASSELL

DEDICATION

This book is dedicated to my dad, Nobby, whose jam fritters I adored,
and my mother-in-law, Joan, who made the best 'Scouse' in Liverpool.
These two wonderful parents cannot be replaced.

Note
Unless otherwise indicated,
all recipes will serve four people.

This edition first published in the UK 1996 by
Cassell
Wellington House
125 Strand
London
WC2R 0BB

Distributed in the United States by
Sterling Publishing Co. Inc.
387 Park Avenue South
New York, NY 10016
USA

Designer Robert Updegraff
Photographer David George

British Library Cataloguing-in-Publication Data
A catalogue record for this book is available from the British Library

ISBN 0–304–34842–2

Printed and bound in Spain

Contents

Foreword

The late Elizabeth David and Jane Grigson, and Derek Cooper of Radio 4's *The Food Programme* have put their exceptional talents behind the neglected charms of British food. More recently, television chefs have shown what wonderful foodstuffs are available throughout the British Isles. Yet we still refuse to acknowledge the exquisite pleasures of British food.

There are several reasons for this. The first is that when, after the austerities of the Second World War and rationing, British interest in the pleasures of food and wine was re-awakened in the 1960s and 1970s, our culinary hearts were left in Parisian bistros, Tuscan trattorie and tapas bars in the south of Spain. Sadly, Lancashire, Yorkshire and Somerset – however wonderful their produce – do not evoke the same culinary passions.

This interest in food from the Continent occurred alongside a national neglect of the small producers of the kind Tom Bridge spent so much time visiting in the research for this book. While French farmers were offered the protection of a national system, ours were left to struggle for formal recognition and survival. This is only now beginning to change, and the EU, vilified in so many quarters, is beginning to recognize and protect those who produce such delicacies as Shetland lamb, Orkney beef and Jersey potatoes.

Lorraine Soup

Nor was the cause of British food helped, except in isolated circumstances, by our nation's restaurateurs. Because we all believe that the finest British dishes require the best raw ingredients, simply cooked, it has been difficult to put these dishes on a menu at reasonable prices – and I speak as a former restaurateur. Offer the best, and you stand accused of being expensive. Offer anything inferior, and people say that they can remember eating better when they were children or, more damning, that they can do better at home. I know from experience that there is more profit to be made from serving numerous portions of *moules à la crème* than the same number of Morecambe Bay potted shrimps, although I much prefer the latter.

British farmers and food producers have had to face these challenges in a rapidly changing Britain. The food served up and down the nation's high streets today bears little resemblance to that served a generation ago. Although we may be known as 'les rosbifs' in Europe, according to a recent survey commissioned by BiSoDol, the indigestion remedy, 15 per cent of the respondents chose curry as their favourite dish, with only 12 per cent opting for roast beef and Yorkshire pudding. And only just behind roast beef was that other British staple, the Chinese takeaway.

But there is no doubt that the worst is over. National pride in, and enjoyment of, the many ingredients and recipes that Tom Bridge so scrupulously investigates in this book are now rapidly on the increase. Ironically, however, a large part of the revival is due to the fact that British produce is being more readily appreciated outside Britain than within. Producers such as Randolph Hodgson and Jason Hinds, who have nurtured the revival of British farmhouse cheeses from their base at Neal's Yard Dairy, London, find that restaurateurs in America are their most avid customers. Nothing in Paris today is more chic than a Scottish smoked salmon sandwich from Marks & Spencer. And in volume terms the figures are even more impressive: in 1995, according to Food from Britain, sales of British food and drink products overseas topped £10 million, an increase of more than 50 per cent since 1990.

Individual artisan farmers and producers – the equivalents of those we enjoy so much when we visit France, Italy or Spain – cannot, however, be saved by overseas markets. To survive and prosper, to be able to plan for the next generation, they have to be appreciated and enjoyed more often and more regularly by an increasing number in this country. The benefits will be manifold. Not only will we all be able to eat a more varied, well-cared for range of foodstuffs, but the survival of small, individual farmers and producers will ensure a finer, more distinctive countryside, something we can all enjoy, if only from a speeding car or train.

Tom Bridge's book will, I hope, go some way to ensuring that producers from West Sussex to County Tyrone, from Gwent to Dorset, will survive and prosper – for us and for future generations to appreciate.

Nicholas Lander

Introduction

'There is no love sincerer than the love of food.'
Bernard Shaw, 1878

Bridge Over Britain is a compilation of food and pictures from around the British Isles.
My love of the true character of food and of the facts and the stories behind our heritage,
which have been brought together through the eyes of photographer David George, will
make this unique cookery book a prized possession for everyone who is interested in the
food and drink of all parts of rural England, Ireland, Scotland and Wales. I have travelled
throughout the country to bring you the delights and pleasures of the food and drink to
be found in this wonderful land.

I am not a member of the wild mushroom, olive oil and sun-dried tomato brigade
of European chefs. I cook what I enjoy cooking, and I will not be told how to present
the beautiful, robust food of this wonderful country.

I wrote this cookery book for the sheer pleasure of being involved in my first love,
British food, and this is my personal choice of some of the best British recipes that can be
found. I have tried to cover all areas and counties, and in each section I have included my
own classic recipe: try my Cucumber Soup with Basil and Mint or Wiltshire Cheese and
Ham Bites for a savoury. There are recipes from the West Country – Avon, Devon and
Cornwall, famed for clotted cream teas, Dorset, with its remarkable Blue Vinny cheese,
Gloucester, Wiltshire, renowned for its pigs, and the famous cider cup of Somerset. From
the southeast there are recipes from Bedford, Buckingham, Oxford – marmalade country
– the Isle of Wight, Berkshire, Hampshire, Hertfordshire, East and West Sussex and the
heart of Surrey. West of Bristol is the home of Caerphilly cheese and the Glamorgan
sausage. Cardigan Bay is full of fresh fish, and we have recipes from Powys, Gwent,
Clewd and Dyfed, from Aberystwyth and Welshpool. I travelled through the Midlands,
from Hereford, Northampton, where I looked at the famous Melton Mowbray pie, and
on to Leicester, Salop, Stafford and to Nottingham, Derby and Cheshire, a county that is
steeped in history.

I visited the eastern counties, from the Essex coastline, north to Suffolk and the
Norfolk broads towards the home of my favourite sausages in Lincolnshire and then on
to Humberside. From there, I went to Northumberland, Yorkshire and its famed pudding, Tyne and Wear, Greater Manchester, Merseyside – the home of Lobscouse and the
Everton mint – my home county of Lancashire, where Sir-loin of Beef was knighted, to
the famous Cumbrian coast, with a wealth of foods and Kendal mint cake – not to men-
tion William Wordsworth and Beatrix Potter – before visiting the Isle of Man where I
tasted the kippers.

Scotland's unforgettable foods include salmon and game, of course, but also Arbroath Smokies, cakes, like Jura and Dundee, and fruits, like the loganberry, tayberry and fresh raspberries. Then my journey took me to Northern Ireland and the Counties of Fermanagh, Armagh, Down, Londonderry, Antrim and Tyrone – the home of Ulster bacon and of my favourite whisky, Bushmills.

My pie recipes include some traditional Victorian dishes. Here are recipes for such famous pies as Cumberland Bacon and Egg, Melton Mowbray, Huntingdon Fidget and Aylesbury Game to name just a few.

Nearly all my life I have been involved with the traditional food of England, whether it be a new or an old recipe. I have spent several years creating ideas for new recipes using British ingredients and re-creating them for television and food manufacturers to take account of the current concern for healthy eating. I have developed recipes for several major food companies that you will have bought in your local store to take home to cook for yourself or your partner.

Developing recipes is very hard work and requires a degree of artistic skill, but my enjoyment lies in seeing the faces of my friends and family when they ask, 'Have you tried the Chicken in Red Wine at this or that superstore?' 'I hope so,' I say. 'I spent six months developing the product.' Throughout the book I have included some of my own 'New English' recipes so that you also can enjoy at first hand the recipes that I hope one day will become our modified favourite English cookery dishes.

Anyone who thinks there is little more to British cooking than mint sauce and fish and chips has only to glance through these pages to see how many truly wonderful British recipes there really are.

SOUPS

Cullen Skink

Irish Potato and Parsley Soup

Welsh Leek Soup – Cawl Cennin

Salcombe Bay Crab Soup

Game Soup with Sherry

Neep and Haggis Soup

Summer Cucumber Soup with Basil and Mint

Cream of Lemon and Chicken Soup

Eighteenth-century Green Pea Soup

Soup was always part of the dinner in the Victorian household, and dinner, being the grand, solid meal of the day, was a matter of considerable importance. 'A well-served table is a striking index of human ingenuity and resource,' said Mrs Beeton in *All about Cookery*. She went on to say:

> The elegance with which a dinner is served depends, of course, partly upon the means, but still more upon the taste of the master and mistress of the house. It may be observed in general, that there should always be flowers on the table, and as they form no item of expense where a garden is, there is no reason why they should not be employed every day.
>
> The variety of the dishes which furnish forth a modern dinner-table [the 1860s] does not necessarily imply anything unwholesome or anything capricious. Food that is not well relished cannot be digested; and the appetite of the overworked man of business, or statesman, or of any dweller in towns, whose occupations are exciting and exhausting must suit their mode of dining to their mode of living.

If that applied in today's world, dinners would be very small.

Every dinner included some form of soup or broth. The Prince Regent loved game soup, but he started his meals with caviar and finished them with Rosa Lewis's famous Quail Pudding.

Soup has always been part of the British diet, and we must be the soup lovers of the world. There are hundreds to choose from, and I have picked the favourites from around the coastlines, towns and villages of our wonderful country. The great chefs and cooks of the British Isles all had one thing in common: they never threw away the water in which meat, fish or vegetables had been boiled. This is the basis for good stock for soups and sauces.

Cullen Skink

Cullen Skink

Cullen is a fishing village on the Moray Firth, and skink means soup, stock or broth. This recipe dates back to when the Moray Firth smokerie used oak chippings from the old whisky barrels to add a unique flavour to smoked finnan haddock. One recipe I created years ago was Haddock Tams Brigg in a 'Taste of Scotland' cookery competition in Ayrshire ... yes, I did win, but I was given a tankard full of the taste of Scotland and cannot remember the rest of the evening or what happened to the tankard.

350g/12oz smoked finnan haddock, skinned
600ml/1pt water
600ml/1pt milk
450g/1lb potatoes, cooked and sliced
salt and freshly ground black pepper

25g/1oz butter
75ml/3fl oz double cream (optional)

Garnish
flaked haddock

• Place the haddock in a large saucepan, cover with boiling water and simmer for about 6 minutes. Remove the bones from the fish and discard them. Return the fish to the stock and boil for 20 minutes. Reserve a little haddock for garnishing.
• Flake the haddock, strain the stock, then add the milk, potatoes and the flaked fish. Simmer for 15 minutes, adjusting the seasoning, adding the butter and a little cream should you wish. Garnish with parsley and serve with white crusty bread.

Irish Potato and Parsley Soup

I was taught how to make this in Dublin by Paul Christopher several years ago. The potato has been part of the Irish diet for centuries, and this recipe originally comes from the beautiful area of Moira in County Down.

3 rashers smoked streaky bacon, rindless and
   chopped
25g/1oz best butter
450g/1lb King Edward potatoes, chopped
450g/1lb onion, chopped

600ml/1pt chicken stock
600ml/1pt fresh milk
150ml/¼pt double cream
salt and freshly ground black pepper
freshly chopped parsley

• Fry the bacon in its own fat in a large saucepan for 4 minutes. Add the butter, potatoes and onion and cook for 12 minutes, stirring all the time. Add the stock and milk, bring to the boil and simmer for 20 minutes.
• Blend in the cream, season and simmer for 5 minutes, add the parsley and serve with Irish soda bread.

Welsh Leek Soup

CAWL CENNIN

The flavour of this soup can be enhanced with a strong Spanish onion and about 900g/2lb of boiled lamb bones, which should be simmered for at least 4 hours. Brian Cashman, who has a bookshop called Cooking the Books in Gwent, tells me that this recipe dates back to 1675 and was often served with Welsh oatcakes.

25g/1oz butter
450g/1lb leeks, trimmed, sliced and washed
350g/12oz onion, chopped
2 celery sticks, chopped
1.2l/2pt lamb stock

salt and freshly ground black pepper
100ml/4fl oz double cream

Garnish
chives, chopped

- Melt the butter in a large saucepan, add the leeks, onion and celery and cook gently for 10 minutes. Add the lamb stock and simmer for 30 minutes.
- Season to taste, add the cream, re-heat and serve with chopped chives.

Salcombe Bay Crab Soup

I had this soup at the Anchor Inn at Star Cross, near Dawlish, Devon, and to say it was good, would be an understatement. Devonshire crabs are very large, and the combination of their rich meat, sherry and cream make this a soup to remember.

50g/2oz butter
1 large onion, sliced
225g/8oz fresh crab meat
25g/1oz plain flour
1.2l/2pt fish stock

salt and freshly ground black pepper
1 tbsp anchovy essence
grated rind and juice of 1 orange
50ml/2fl oz dry sherry
275ml/½pt double cream

- Melt the butter in a large saucepan, add the onion and crab meat and cook gently for 6 minutes. Add the flour, stirring thoroughly to avoid lumps. Very slowly add the fish stock, stirring all the time until the soup comes to the boil, and allow it to simmer for 40 minutes.
- Season with salt and freshly ground black pepper, and add the anchovy essence, orange juice and rind, sherry and cream.
- Re-heat and serve with crusty brown bread and a dry white wine.

Game Soup with Sherry

This recipe is served in most game shooting areas of Britain, and for some reason it is very popular with the golfing fraternity, too. These days game can be bought in most super-markets and it can be purchased ready cut and trimmed. For an extra boost to this recipe, add some fresh cranberry juice, replacing about half of the meat stock with the juice.

50g/2oz butter
1 onion, peeled and diced
1 carrot, peeled and diced
1 celery stick, diced
450g/1lb venison, fat removed and diced
450g/1lb any game meat (rabbit, pheasant or grouse), diced

50g/2oz plain flour
1l/1¾pt meat stock
1 bay leaf
8 black peppercorns
pinch of salt
3 tbsp redcurrant jelly
150ml/¼pt cream sherry

• Melt the butter in a saucepan, add the onion, carrot, celery and meat, cook slowly for 6 minutes, then sprinkle with flour.
• Cook for a further 2 minutes and slowly add the stock with the bay leaf, pepper-corns and salt. Simmer for 1 hour. Add the redcurrant jelly and sherry, let the soup stand for at least 4 hours. Remove the bay leaf and put the stock and game meat through a blender or liquidizer.
• Re-heat and simmer for 10 minutes. Serve with croutons.

George at the Hart of England Deer Farm, Warwickshire.

Neep and Haggis Soup

Steve Johnstone, of the Dalhousie Castle, Bonnyrigg, near Edinburgh, created the recipe especially for this book. It is basically turnip soup, but flavoured with haggis, whisky and cream. The haggis already contains plenty of seasoning, so there is no need for extra salt and pepper.

50g/2oz butter
450g/1lb turnips, peeled and diced
1 large onion, chopped
1 large potato, peeled and chopped
1 tbsp parsley

1l/1¾pt chicken stock
1 small haggis, about 225g/8oz
4 tbsp malt whisky
300ml/½pt double cream

• In a large saucepan melt the butter and add the turnip, onion and potato. Cook over a low heat for 10 minutes and add the parsley and chicken stock. Cover and simmer for 40 minutes until the vegetables are soft.
• Add the haggis by crumbling it into the soup. Cook for 10 minutes, then put it into a blender or food processor and purée until the soup has a smooth texture.
• Return the soup to the pan, add the whisky and half the cream and slowly heat through. Garnish with a swirl of cream and fresh nasturtium flowers. Serve with crusty brown bread and a wee dram.

Summer Cucumber Soup
WITH BASIL AND MINT

I created this soup for some friends during the Newburgh Village Fair several years ago, basing it on a recipe that originated from Nantwich, Cheshire. If you do not like cucumber try beetroot – the flavour is excellent and very different from other soups. Simple, light and easy to make, serve it hot or cold. The soup is excellent for a summer party, and you can give it a little more punch by allowing it to cool, then adding a little Crème de Menthe.

2 large cucumbers
50g/2oz rapeseed oil
1 tsp clear honey
4 sprigs of fresh basil
4 sprigs of fresh mint
25g/1oz plain flour
300ml/½pt fresh milk
300ml/½pt vegetable stock (cube)

1 orange, juice and zest
salt and freshly ground black pepper
4 tbsp fromage frais

Garnish
basil, freshly chopped
mint, freshly chopped
cucumber skin, grated

- Carefully grate the skin from the cucumbers and place to one side for the garnish. Remove the centre seeds and discard them. Finely chop the cucumbers and place to one side.
- Put 25g/1oz of the rapeseed oil into a saucepan and heat. Add the cucumber, honey, sprigs of basil and mint. Cover and cook for 10 minutes.
- In another saucepan heat the remaining rapeseed oil and add the flour, stirring for 1 minute. Slowly add the milk until it turns into a smooth white sauce, and add this to the cucumbers with the vegetable stock, orange juice and zest.
- Thoroughly blend everything together and allow the soup to simmer for at least 20 minutes, stirring every 3 minutes.
- Remove the mint and basil stalks and purée in a blender or pass through a fine sieve.
- Re-heat, season and add the fromage frais. Pour into a soup tureen and sprinkle with the chopped basil, mint and the grated cucumber.

Cream of Lemon and Chicken Soup

The unique flavour of this soup is a real taste of Victorian England. When I was visiting Belfast I came across the Irish version, which includes orange and lemon and uses chicken stock. Another alternative is to replace the lemons with oranges and the chicken with breast of duckling meat (skin removed) for an Orange and Duck Soup.

50g/2oz butter
8 shallots, skinned and thinly sliced
2 medium sized carrots, peeled and thinly sliced
2 celery sticks, washed and thinly sliced
225g/8oz breast of chicken meat, finely
    chopped (skin removed)
3 lemons

1.2l/2pt chicken stock
salt and freshly ground white pepper
150ml/¼pt fresh double cream

Garnish
sprig of parsley
slices of lemon

• In a large saucepan melt the butter, add the vegetables and chicken meat and cook gently for 8 minutes.

• Thinly pare the lemons, blanch the lemon rind in boiling water for 3 minutes, then add the rind and freshly squeezed lemon juice to the pan with the chicken stock. Bring slowly to the boil and simmer for 50 minutes.

• Cool the soup and put it through a blender. Return the soup to the saucepan, re heat, season and add the cream. Do not boil or the soup will curdle.

• Pour the soup into a tureen or individual bowls, add a sprig of parsley and a half slice of lemon. Serve with Irish soda bread with lashings of butter

Eighteenth-century Green Pea Soup

In 1932 Florence White wrote a marvellous book called *Good Things in England*, and this recipe was in it. I have converted it to modern weights for your use, and I am sure you will find it well worth the two guineas Madame Parker gave for the 'receipt' in the eighteenth century. At Henley-on-Thames during the regatta the soup stall sold a bowl of thick green broth for ½ d – if you had a lump of bread, too, it cost 3 farthings.

25g/1oz butter
125g/4oz rindless smoked bacon, diced
2 celery sticks, diced
1 onion, sliced
600ml/1pt fresh milk
600ml/1pt meat stock
450g/1lb ready soaked peas

sprig of fresh mint
1 cos lettuce, shredded
salt and freshly ground black pepper
1 cucumber, de-seeded and cut into small dice
1 cauliflower, cooked and made into florets
    (warm)

• Melt the butter in a large saucepan, add the bacon, celery and onion and cook for 5 minutes.

• Add the milk, stock, peas, mint and shredded lettuce and season well. Bring to the boil and simmer for 35 minutes. Sieve or strain the soup.

• Float the cucumber and cauliflower florets on the soup and serve with warm crusty bread.

SAVOURIES

Tom's Black Pudding and Potato with Mustard Sauce
Morecambe Bay Potted Shrimps
Potted Stilton
Yorkshire Goat's Cheese Tartlet
Wiltshire Cheese and Ham Bites
Toad in th'Hole
Quire of Paper
Birmingham Bacon Cakes
Glamorgan Sausages – Selsigen Morgannwg
Marinated Manx Kipper Fillets
Welsh Rarebit – Caws Pobi
Scotch Eggs
Cheshire Cheese Cakes with Creamed Leeks in Sherry Vinegar
Eggy Bread
Scotch Smoked Salmon and Scrambled Eggs
The Perfect Cheese Omelette
Yorkshire Potted Smoked Fillet of Trout
Solomongundy
A Delicious Savoury
Scotch Woodcock
Norwich Creamed Veal Kidneys

The Spanish have *tapas*, the French have the hors-d'oeuvre and the British have savouries. This selection includes just a few of some of the tastiest recipes for this neglected group. Try them for an excellent light lunch, supper or small buffet when your friends come to visit.

The Far-famed Black Pudding

TAKE groats and pearl barley, tie it up loosely in a bag and boil until cooked, place in a large tub and add seasoning, flour and onions chopped. Mix well whilst hot. Add cubes of back fat or leaf cut into quarter inch squares. Now add the blood and stiffen with oatmeal.

Fill into a bullock runner with pudding filler, allowing about 6 to 8 pieces of fat to each pudding. Tie up firmly and boil gently for about 20 minutes.

Thornley's Pork Butchers, Chorley, 1920

Black Pudding and Potato

Tom's Black Pudding

AND POTATO WITH MUSTARD SAUCE

Sauce is the soul of food, and I am sure you will appreciate this very novel recipe, which comes from Lancashire.

4 rings of fat-free black pudding
4 large potatoes, peeled, boiled and thickly sliced
50g/2oz butter
2 onions, peeled and thinly sliced
2 apples, peeled, cored and sliced
50g/2oz plain flour

100ml/3fl oz coarse grain mustard
1 tbsp English mustard
300ml/9fl oz meat stock
pinch of nutmeg
pinch of thyme
salt and freshly ground black pepper
100g/4oz Cheddar cheese, grated

• Pre-heat the oven to 200°C/400°F/gas mark 6.
• Cut the black pudding into slices 2.5cm/1in thick. Remove any skin from the black pudding. Line a deep baking dish with the slices of potato.
• In a saucepan fry the onions in the butter, remove the onions with a slotted spoon, retaining the butter in the pan for later. Place the onions over the potato, covering them completely.
• Add the slices of apple to the base of the dish so that they cover the onions, then finish off with the black pudding.
• Put the flour and mustards into the pan in which the onions had been fried and cook for 2 minutes. Slowly add the stock, stirring constantly until the sauce is smooth. Sprinkle with nutmeg and thyme, taste and season with salt and pepper.
• Finally pour the sauce over the black pudding, sprinkle with grated cheese and bake in the oven for 20 minutes.

Morecambe Bay Potted Shrimps

The best shrimps to use for this recipe are the small brown ones that have come from Morecambe Bay for hundreds of years. They became very popular during the Victorian period, when visitors from all over England visited the resort for their traditional Easter and summer breaks. This is a quick and simple recipe, but it is very important that you do not boil the shrimps – heat them gently and slowly.

450g/1lb Morecambe Bay shrimps
225g/8oz softened butter
generous pinch of nutmeg
generous pinch cayenne pepper
salt and freshly ground black pepper

100g/4oz clarified butter (see page 21)

Garnish
1 lemon cut into wedges

- Place the ingredients (apart from the clarified butter) into a pan and heat gently, making sure they do not boil. Stir carefully until well coated with butter.
- Place the shrimps in individual ramekins or one small potting dish and cover with clarified butter.
- Allow them to cool for 2 hours, garnish with fresh lemon and serve with thinly sliced buttered brown bread or warm toast.

Clarified Butter

Place 225g/8oz fresh unsalted butter in a saucepan and heat very slowly, skimming off the foam as it heats up. The sediment will sink to the bottom of the pan as the butter heats.

When the butter has completely melted, remove the pan from the heat and leave it to stand for 2 minutes, allowing the sediment to settle on the bottom. Very slowly and carefully pour the clarified butter into a small container, leaving the sediment in the pan. The butter is then ready to be poured over the surface of your potted dishes.

Potted Stilton

Being a great lover of cheese, I really enjoy this type of recipe. Stilton is potted quite regularly and it is available at most superstores, but it was Richard Dolby, cook at the Thatched House Tavern in St James's Street, London, who served his recipe to the customers with a jug of porter.

Potted Cheshire cheese was introduced around 1700, and in the 1740s Hannah Glasse produced her version in the *Art of Cookery*.

To Pot Cheshire Cheese

Take three pounds of Cheshire Cheese, and put it into a mortar, with half a pound of the best fresh Butter you can get. Pound them together, and in the beating add a Gill of rich Canary Wine and half an ounce of Mace finely beat, then sifted fine like a fine powder. When all is extremely well mixed, press it hard down in a Gallipot. Cover it with clarified Butter, and keep it cool.

A slice of this exceeds all the Cream Cheese that can be made.

450g/1lb mellow Stilton	2 tbsp port
100g/4oz unsalted butter, softened	
generous pinch of powdered mace	100g/4oz clarified butter
1 tsp English mustard	

- Mash all the ingredients together thoroughly or blend in a blender until it becomes very creamy in texture.
- Place the mixture into earthenware or ramekin dishes, making sure that the cheese is pressed down firmly.
- Top with clarified butter and place into the refrigerator for at least 2 days.
- Serve with fresh Eccles Cakes (see page 121), toast or fresh bread.

Yorkshire Goat's Cheese Tartlet

This is a quick, simple recipe, which I have converted from the one used at the Worsley Arms, Hovingham, where it is usually served as individual tartlets with leeks, buttered spinach and deep-fried chives, as shown below.

1 pie case, pre-cooked, baked blind
25g/1oz butter
250g/8oz fresh spinach leaves, stalks removed
  and washed
salt
4 tbsp single cream

250g/8oz Yorkshire goat's cheese
3 egg yolks
freshly ground black pepper
1 tbsp chopped chives
freshly grated nutmeg

• Pre-heat the oven to 200°C/400°F/gas mark 6. Make the pie case and put it to one side.

• Melt the butter in a saucepan and add the washed spinach, season with salt and cook for 3 minutes, add the cream, simmer and cook for 5–6 minutes, until the spinach is liquid free.

• Meanwhile, in a clean bowl thoroughly blend the goat's cheese, egg yolks, pepper and chives. Place the spinach in the base of the pie case, top with the goat's cheese mixture, grate over some fresh nutmeg and bake in the centre of the oven for 25 minutes.

Wiltshire Cheese and Ham Bites

This is a novel way of using up ends of cheese, ham, chicken, bacon, meat and so on. The recipe is one of those that everyone had to use during the war, when it was a case of never throwing anything away.

50g/2oz butter or margarine
8 tbsp water
100g/4oz flour
4 eggs
50g/2oz Cheddar cheese, grated

50g/2oz York ham or cooked chicken, chopped
1 small onion, finely chopped
salt and freshly ground black pepper

corn oil for deep frying

• In a saucepan bring the butter and water to the boil and remove from the heat. Add the flour, stirring briskly until the mixture forms a soft ball. Cool slightly.
• Slowly add the eggs, beating them until the mixture becomes smooth. Add the rest of the ingredients, mixing well.
• Drop small teaspoons of the mixture into the hot fat, frying each one for 4 minutes until they are golden-brown.

> You can use your favourite cheese with this recipe. I really enjoy Stilton and grated pear, served with a glass of port. Vegetarians could use their favourite shredded vegetables.

Caviar was very expensive in the early nineteenth century, and this recipe for Mock Caviar appeared from a Dr Hunter from York in 1806.

TAKE anchovies, parsley and chives or shallots. Pound them in a marble mortar, with some olive-oil, salt and lemon juice. Make a toast of white bread and spread the mixture upon it. Cut it into neat pieces and serve it up.

He then goes on to say: 'This is a very good substitute for Caviar.'

Toad in th'Hole

Toad in th'Hole is something of a national institution today, but years ago beef, chicken, goat and even fish were used, not the Great British banger. My preference is for Cumberland sausage, but you can try cooked meats instead if you like. If possible, make the batter the day before and let it settle.

450g/1lb fresh Cumberland sausage, cut into
   5cm/2in pieces
30ml/1fl oz corn oil

Yorkshire pudding batter
100g/4oz plain flour
pinch of salt
1 large fresh egg
200ml/7fl oz fresh milk
100ml/3fl oz cold water

- Pre-heat the oven to 220°C/425°F/gas mark 7.
- Place the sausage pieces in a deep baking tray with the oil and bake for 10 minutes.
- Meanwhile make the batter. Mix the flour and a pinch of salt in a bowl, then make a well in the centre and break in the egg. Add half the milk and, using a wooden spoon, work it into the flour to form a paste, beating the mixture until it is smooth. Slowly add the rest of the milk and then the water. Beat until it is a smooth consistency.
- Remove the hot tray from the oven, pour the batter over the sausages and return the tray to the oven for 20–30 minutes until the batter is risen and golden-brown.
- Serve with a rich onion gravy or a light potato salad.

Add 1 tbsp of caster sugar to the batter and place 4 pears, peeled, cored and halved, on a tray with 25g/1oz butter. Cook using the same method.

OTHER USES FOR YORKSHIRE PUDDING BATTER

I thought you might be quite amused to read the following recipe from my cookery book collection:

PANCAKES. Make a light batter of eggs, flour and milk. Fry it in a small pan, in hot corn oil or lard. Salt, nutmeg or ginger may be added. Sugar and lemon should be served to eat with them. When eggs are very scarce, the batter may be made of flour and small beer, with the addition of a little ginger; or clean snow with flour and a very little milk, will serve instead of an egg!

The Cook and Housekeepers' Dictionary, 1823

I have revised the traditional recipe for modern use. I use fresh strawberries, tossed in caster sugar and a little Drambuie and a double thick cream for the fillings.

100g/4oz plain flour
25g/1oz caster sugar
2 eggs with 2 extra egg yolks
150ml/¼pt fresh milk

150ml/¼pt single cream
4 tbsp sherry

butter for frying

MAKES 8–10 PANCAKES

• Sieve the flour and sugar into a large, clean bowl. Beat together the eggs, yolks, milk and cream and pour the mixture onto the flour, whisking briskly until you have a very smooth batter. Then add the sherry, whisking briskly again.
• Let the batter settle for 30 minutes, then whisk briskly again before using.
• Heat a heavy non-stick omelette or pancake pan, brush generously with melted butter and fry the pancakes in the normal way.
• Create your own filling, using fruit, redcurrant jelly, jam or ice cream with butter-scotch, grated chocolate, purée of apple and cinnamon, honey, lemon and sugar or even fruit yoghurt.

Quire of Paper

Mary Kettilby, 1728, and Ann Peckham from Leeds, 1700, used this recipe for Quire of Paper or Thin Cream Pancakes.

TAKE to a pint of Cream, eight eggs, leaving out two whites, three spoonfuls of fine flour, three spoonfuls of sack (sherry) and one spoonful of orange flower water, a little sugar, a grated nutmeg and a quart of a pound of butter, melted in the cream. Mingle all well together, mixing the flour with a little cream at first, that it may be smooth. Butter your pan for the first pan-cake, and let them run as thin as you can possibly to be whole. When one side is colour'd tis enough. Take them carefully out of the pan and strew some fine sifted sugar between each; lay them as even on each other as you can. This quantity will make twenty.

Birmingham Bacon Cakes

A lot of lovely food – including one of my favourites, Bourneville chocolate –
comes from this area of the country. Brummy Cakes were served at
country fairs in late Victorian times.

100g/4oz rindless streaky bacon
225g/8oz self-raising flour
salt
25g/1oz butter
75g/3oz Cheddar Cheese, grated

freshly ground black pepper
150 ml/5fl oz milk
1 tbsp tomato ketchup
1 tsp Worcestershire sauce
1 tbsp milk for glazing

SERVES 8

• Pre-heat the oven to 200°C/400°F/gas mark 6.
• Grill the bacon until it is crisp and cut it into small pieces.
• Sieve the flour and a pinch of salt together, add the butter and rub in finely. Add
the bacon, one-third of the cheese and pepper.
• Mix the milk, ketchup and Worcestershire sauce and add to the dry ingredients
to make a soft dough.
• On a floured board roll out a circle about 18cm/7in across. Brush with milk
and cut into 8 wedges. Arrange these on a greased baking sheet and sprinkle with
the remaining cheese. Bake in the centre of the oven for 20 minutes.
• Serve garnished with watercress.

Glamorgan Sausages
SELSIGEN MORGANNWG

This cheese-flavoured savoury takes its name from the shape of the food –
not from the ingredients.

pinch of mixed herbs
pinch of mustard
a little finely chopped onion
150g/5oz fresh white breadcrumbs
75g/3oz Caerphilly cheese, grated

salt and freshly ground black pepper
1 egg, separated
plain flour
75g/3oz crisp breadcrumbs for frying
oil for shallow frying

• Mix together the herbs, mustard, onion, breadcrumbs and cheese and season
well. Bind together with the yolk of an egg.
• Divide the mixture into small sausage shapes and roll in the flour. Dip each
sausage into the white of the egg and roll in breadcrumbs. Fry the sausages in hot
oil for 5 minutes until they are golden-brown.
• Serve hot with potatoes or cold with a fresh green salad.

Marinated Manx Kipper Fillets

The Isle of Man has always been famous for oak-smoked kipper fillets. More recently it is
known as the home of the famous T.T. races and of Nigel Mansell, who really does like this
recipe when it is made with crushed cloves of garlic and a little cayenne pepper sprinkled
over. Other masters of the kipper world are, of course, the curers at Loch Fyne in Scotland.

6 oak-smoked Manx kipper fillets, uncooked

Marinade
1 tsp dry English mustard
1 clove of garlic, crushed
3 tbsp ground nut oil
1 tbsp tarragon vinegar
2 shallots, finely sliced

1 tbsp parsley, freshly chopped
juice of 1 lemon
freshly ground black pepper

Garnish
1 lemon, sliced
2 sprigs of washed parsley

• Cut each kipper fillet diagonally into 5 strips, following the natural grain of the fillet.
• Put all the ingredients for the marinade into a clean bowl and blend with a
wooden spoon. Place the fillets in the marinade and leave in a refrigerator for 12
hours.
• Place the fillets on a serving dish garnished with lemon and parsley. Serve with
rye bread and a fresh watercress salad.

Welsh Rarebit

CAWS POBI

✦

One of my favourite authors is Elizabeth David, and she wrote the following letter to a newspaper in 1995.

Welsh Welsh Rabbit

Glynn Christian states that he has found no recipes for Welsh rabbit/rarebit which suggest Welsh cheese. If he were to refer to Lady Llanover's *Good Cookery*, published in 1867, he would find an authentic recipe, as follows:

> 'Cut a slice of the real Welsh cheese made of sheep and cow's milk, toast it at the fire on both sides, but not so much as to drop; toast a piece of bread, less than a quarter of an inch thick, to be quite crisp, and spread it very thinly with fresh cold butter on one side (it must not be saturated with butter), then lay the toasted cheese upon the bread and serve immediately on a very hot plate; the butter can, of course, be omitted.'

Lady Llanover's husband, formerly Sir Benjamin Hall, was MP for Newport in south Wales. The story goes that Big Ben was named after him.

Elizabeth David, London SW3

✦

225g/8oz Gloucester, Caerphilly or Cheshire cheese, grated
25g/1oz butter
1 tsp Worcestershire sauce
1 tsp dry English mustard
1 tsp flour
4 tbsp stout
freshly ground black pepper
4 slices bread, toasted on one side only

• Put the cheese, butter, Worcestershire sauce, mustard and flour into a saucepan. Stirring well, add the stout and ground black pepper. Cook and stir continuously over a very gentle heat until smooth.

• Place the mixture on the untoasted side of the bread 'very Caerphilly' and brown under the grill.

Scotch Eggs

Believe it or not, this used to be part of the Scottish breakfast, eaten with other delights such as porridge with whisky, and bacon and fried eggs with sliced fried haggis. Today we serve Scotch eggs with a little mustard for excellent quick lunch and supper snacks. Try Cumberland sausage meat instead of pork for a more robust savoury flavour or Lincolnshire sausage meat if you prefer something a little less spicy.

6 medium size eggs, hard-boiled and shelled
seasoned flour
350g/12oz Cumberland sausage meat
1 tbsp parsley, chopped
2 shallots, finely chopped
little grated nutmeg

pinch of marjoram
pinch of basil
salt and freshly ground black pepper
1 egg beaten with a little milk
100g/4oz freshly toasted breadcrumbs
cooking oil

MAKES 6

- Roll the eggs in the seasoned flour.
- Place the sausage meat in a bowl with the parsley, shallots, nutmeg, marjoram, basil, salt and freshly ground black pepper. Work all the ingredients in together.
- Divide the sausage meat into six equal portions and flatten each into a round. Place an egg on each round and, with wet hands, work the meat around the egg to form a smooth, even layer. Make sure that you seal the meat well. Roll each egg in the egg wash, then in the breadcrumbs.
- Heat the oil and deep fry the eggs for 6 minutes until they are golden-brown, turning them every minute so that they cook evenly. Remove the eggs with a slotted spoon onto some kitchen paper to remove the excess oil.
- Allow them to cool and serve with a sweetcorn salad.

Alpine Eggs

BUTTER a small fireproof dish thickly and line it with the greater part of 6oz cheese cut into slices. Break over four eggs without breaking the yolks; seasoning them with salt and pepper. Grate the remainder of the cheese and mix it with a little chopped parsley. Lay it over the top and over this put some butter in small pieces. Bake it in a quick oven for 10 minutes and serve it hot.

The Book of Household Management, Mrs Beeton, 1861

A Fricassey of Eggs

BOIL eight eggs hard, take off the shells, cut them into quarters, have ready half pint of Cream, and a quarter of a pound of fresh Butter, stir it together over the Fire till it is thick and smooth, lay the eggs in your dish and pour the same over. Garnish with the hard yolks of three eggs cut in two and lay around the edge of the dish.

From *The Art Of Cookery Made Plain And Easy*, Hannah Glasse, 1747

Cheshire Cheese Cakes
WITH CREAMED LEEKS IN SHERRY VINEGAR

At least once a month I pay homage to the heart of Cheshire, principally because I love the cheese. Appleby's Cheshire cheese has a more pronounced taste than any other Cheshire cheese, and it must, if at all possible, be used in this recipe from David Alton.

225g/8oz Cheshire cheese, grated
50g/2oz leeks, finely diced
50g/2oz fresh white breadcrumbs
225g/8oz mashed potato, with a little cream
  and butter
salt and freshly ground white pepper
25g/1oz plain flour for coating
1 egg blended with 2 tbsp milk
75g/3oz toasted breadcrumbs
50g/2oz unsalted butter

2 tbsp corn oil
225g/8oz leeks, sliced into rounds
25g/1oz butter
150ml/¼pt double cream
2 tbsp sherry vinegar
salt and freshly ground black pepper

Garnish
edible flowers
fresh thyme

MAKES 8–10

• Combine the cheese, diced leeks, fresh white breadcrumbs and mashed potato. Season well and shape into 8–10 small but thick cakes, 3cm/1¼in high by about 7cm/3in across. Lightly coat the cakes with flour, then egg liquid and roll onto the toasted breadcrumbs, so that each cake is completely coated.

• Heat the butter and corn oil and gently fry the cheese cakes for 3 minutes either side until golden-brown. Put them on a plate and keep warm.

• Fry the leeks in the butter for 3 minutes, remove the fat and return the leeks to the pan (reserving a few for the garnish), add the cream and slowly cook for 2 minutes. Add the vinegar and seasoning and cook for a further minute. Place the creamed leeks on a large, warm serving dish, arrange the cakes on the leeks and top with fried leeks. Surround with the cream sauce and garnish with edible flowers and thyme. Serve with a glass of apple wine.

Eggy Bread

Every child in Britain must have tasted this at least once in a lifetime. I adored this recipe because any and every type of flavour could be added to the bread – if you use bacon fat and half butter to fry the bread, the flavour of bacon will come through. Make sure the grill is on before you start.

150ml/¼ pt milk
4 fresh eggs
salt and freshly ground black pepper
8 slices of white bread, buttered

100g/4oz red Leicester cheese, grated
25g/1oz butter
25g/1oz bacon fat

- Beat the milk and eggs together, season well with salt and freshly ground black pepper
- Make the bread and cheese up into sandwiches and cut into triangles. Dip them all into the egg mixture and let them soak for a few minutes.
- Melt the butter and bacon fat in a frying pan and fry the bread on both sides until brown. Place them quickly under the grill and serve.

Try this recipe with crispy bacon finely chopped with the grated cheese, or use your favourite fillings – prawns or sausages, perhaps. This recipe is there to be enjoyed.

Shrimp Toast From Lowestoft, 1870

This recipe was devised by a grand old chef's grandfather. Eric Shaw, who lived in Lowestoft, passed this on to his son, also called Eric, who taught me to cook when I was thirteen or fifteen years old.

225g/8oz brown (Morecambe Bay) shrimps
25g/1oz unsalted butter
1 egg, beaten with 1 tbsp cream
salt

pinch of cayenne
anchovy paste
8 slices of toasted brown bread

Put the shrimps with the butter into a saucepan and heat gently. When hot, add the egg and cream, stirring until nearly cooked. Season well with salt and cayenne pepper.

Spread the anchovy paste onto the hot toast and top with the shrimp mixture cut into triangles.

Scotch Smoked Salmon
AND SCRAMBLED EGGS

Only the best Scotch or Irish smoked salmon should be used for this recipe and it should not be cooked with the scrambled egg, which will ruin the flavour of the salmon. The rich and famous still ask for this as a savoury starter for Sunday brunch, served with a glass of Buck's Fizz.

225g/8oz Scotch smoked salmon, seasoned with black pepper
8 fresh eggs
5 tbsp double cream

salt
generous pinch of freshly grated nutmeg
freshly ground black pepper
50g/2oz butter

- Cut the sliced and seasoned smoked salmon into diamond shapes.
- In a large bowl mix together the eggs, cream, salt, nutmeg and pepper, whisking them well.
- Melt the butter slowly in a large, non-stick frying pan, add the egg mixture and, using a wooden spoon, stir all the time until the mixture becomes creamy and is just thickening but is still wet.
- Divide the scrambled egg on warm plates and top with diamonds of smoked salmon.

The Perfect Cheese Omelette

The French make their omelettes flat, but we like ours to rise, and the easiest and lightest way of making an omelette is to use my method.

3 eggs, separated into clean bowls
4 tbsp double cream
salt and freshly ground black pepper
25g/1oz Cheddar cheese, grated
25g/1oz butter

Garnish
sprig of fresh parsley
1 tomato, sliced

SERVES 2

- Beat the egg yolks with 2 tbsp of cream and season. Whisk the egg whites until peaky and gently fold into the egg yolks. Add half the grated cheese.
- Turn the grill to high.
- Melt the butter in a small omelette pan, making sure that the bottom and sides of the pan are coated with the butter and that the pan is hot. Add the mixture and when the omelette is nearly firm but still slightly wet, add the rest of the cream and cheese.
- Brown quickly under the grill until the omelette rises and slide onto a warm plate. Garnish with a little parsley and sliced tomato.

This method can be used for a soufflé omelette. If you want a flat omelette, do not separate the eggs and do not place under a hot grill.

Omelettes or Pan-fried Eggs

These eggs were mentioned in one of the very first cookery books, *The Forme of Cury*, c.1385, which was compiled by the master cooks of Richard II. Several early works have led me to believe that the 'amulet' was discovered in England and not in France.

> TAKE some Egges and beat them well with a little faire water and salt, then take a frying pan and melt your Butter: and then put in your Egges, then take a knife and lift up your Egges, that the raw may goe all to the bottom of the pan, then turne it up with your knife on every side that it may become square, then lay a dish upon the pan, and then turne the pan upside down upon the dish and so serue in your Egges with Verinyce and Vinegar, which you will.
>
> *The Forme of Cury*, c.1385

As I am sure you can see, this is an omelette sprinkled with 'verjuice' or vinegar. 'Verjuice', which is mentioned frequently in old cookery books, is a form of distilled apple juice – what today we would call cider vinegar.

Baked Omelette

Butter a small pie dish, Beat 2 new-laid eggs with 1 tbsp of milk, a little salt and pepper.

Pour into the dish, and bake in a moderate oven [180°C/350°F/gas mark 4] until set. Time five to ten minutes according to heat of oven.

Florence White, 1924

Amulet of Asparagus

Beat up six eggs with cream, boil some of the large and finest asparagus. When boiled, cut off all the green in small pieces. Mix them with the eggs and put in some pepper and salt. Make a slice of butter hot in the pan, put them in, and serve them on buttered toast.

1806

Yorkshire Potted Smoked Fillet of Trout

Over the last year I have been giving advice on several smoked products, including venison, ostrich and even kangaroo meat. Trout, however, is one of the most versatile smoked products that we have, and you can use it in almost any recipe that requires fish. During my tour of Britain I visited Harrogate, where I met one of the leading authorities on trout, Robin Scott, who, with Jurg Bleiker, enjoys the pleasures of smoking not just fish but anything that needs smoking.

100g/4oz butter
6 smoked trout fillets
100g/4oz creamed cheese
1 tsp horseradish, freshly grated
freshly ground black pepper
1 tbsp lemon juice

Garnish
8 lemon slices
10 black olives, stoned
100g/4oz smoked salmon

• Beat the butter with 4 of the trout fillets, add the creamed cheese, horseradish, freshly ground black pepper and lemon juice and blend thoroughly. Roughly chop the remaining trout fillets and interlayer the mixtures of smooth and rough trout into small individual buttered pots or one large earthenware dish.

• Top with slices of lemon and olives. Cut the smoked salmon into small diamond shapes and arrange around the edge of the pots or dish. Chill for 4 hours and serve with homemade bread and a glass of chilled white wine.

Solomongundy
SALLID MAGUNDI

This dish originates from Tudor times, and I have about fourteen different recipes with three different ways of spelling the name. This is an excellent recipe for a barbecue party or for that special evening when you want to serve something extra but don't know what!

Salmagundy

I have devised a modern version, but I thought you might like to see another recipe, so here is Mrs Glasse's original recipe for Salmagundy, which dates from 1747.

1. Take 2 pickled herrings and bone them; a handful of parsley, four eggs boiled hard, the meat of one roasted chicken or fowl.
2. Chop all very fine separately, that is the yolks of eggs by themselves, and the whites the same.
3. Scrape some lean boiled ham and hung beef very fine.
4. Turn a small china basin or deep saucer upside down in your dish.
5. Make some butter into the shape of a pineapple, or any other shape you please, and set on the top of the basin or saucer.
6. Lay round the basin a ring of shred parsley, then white of eggs, then ham, then chicken, then beef, then yolks of eggs, then herrings, till you have covered the basin and used all your ingredients.
7. Garnish the dish with whole capers and pickles of any sort you choose, chopped fine.
8. Or you may leave out the butter and put the ingredients in the basin and put a flower of any sort at the top, or a sprig of myrtle.

---

1 large flat lettuce
8 rollmop herrings and juice
4 x 150g/6oz chicken breast, cooked and thinly sliced
6 hard-boiled eggs, quartered
100g/4oz York ham, sliced
100g/4oz roast beef, sliced
100g/4oz roast lamb, sliced
150g/6oz mange tout, cooked and cooled
100g/4oz seedless black grapes

20 stuffed olives, sliced
12 shallots, peeled and boiled
50g/2oz flaked almonds
50g/2oz sultanas

Garnish
2 oranges, zested and sliced
sprig of fresh mint leaves
salt and freshly ground black pepper

• Take a large, flat, oval platter and completely cover it with lettuce. Then, starting with the herrings, line the platter, lengthways from the top, using the herrings, chicken, eggs and meats. Cover the platter completely, then line between each item of food with the mange tout, sliced grapes, olives, shallots, almonds and sultanas.
• Finally, garnish with a sprinkling of orange zest, slices of orange and mint leaves. Season well with salt and freshly ground black pepper.
• Pour the juice over the herrings and serve with fresh crusty bread.
• If you wish, garnish with cold, cooked vegetables such as sliced beans, baby sweetcorn and beetroot, or with red cabbage, which always looks good.

A Delicious Savoury

Long before quiches became fashionable we had our own idea of what a quiche would look like if it were rolled up. We came up with this wonderful idea in the 1900s ... then along came the French and flattened it out!

225g/8oz self-raising flour
1 tsp baking powder
pinch of salt
100g/4oz shredded vegetable suet
water
25g/1oz corn oil
3 onions, peeled and sliced

8 rashers smoked middle bacon, rindless
175g/6oz Irish Cheddar cheese, grated
100g/4oz cooked mashed potato
1 egg blended with 2 tbsp double cream
salt and freshly ground black pepper
1 tsp sage, chopped
1 egg, beaten, for glaze

• Pre-heat the oven to 375°F/190°C/gas mark 5.
• Sift the flour, baking powder and salt into a large mixing bowl, blend in the suet and slowly add sufficient water to make a stiff dough. Flour a board and roll out the dough to an oblong, 30 x 15cm/12 x 6in.
• Heat the oil and fry the onions and bacon until cooked – about 6 minutes – allow the bacon to cool and then roughly chop.
• Place the bacon and onion in a clean bowl and add the cheese, potato, egg and cream, salt and freshly ground black pepper. Blend the mixture well until it is creamy but firm, then put it on the pastry. Sprinkle with sage.
• Brush the sides of the pastry with beaten egg then roll it into an oblong (Swiss roll style), sealing the ends.
• Make 3 diagonal cuts into the top of the pastry and place on a lightly greased baking sheet. Place in the centre of the oven and bake for 50–60 minutes until golden-brown.

Scotch Woodcock

This recipe was first introduced in the second quarter of the nineteenth century, and it certainly reflects the quality of British cookery during this period.

4 slices medium or thick bread
50g/2oz soft butter
8 anchovies
4 eggs

150ml/¼pt double cream
freshly ground black pepper and salt
pinch of cayenne pepper (optional)

- Toast the bread and butter well on both sides.
- Wash and scrape the anchovies, then spread 4 between 2 slices of toast. Repeat with the other 4. Beat the yolks of the eggs with the cream and season well (add a small pinch of cayenne if you wish). Pour the liquid slowly into a saucepan and heat gently, taking care to thicken it without allowing it to boil. Remove the saucepan from the heat.
- Pour the liquid over the pieces of toast and serve immediately.
- For the more health-conscious, fromage frais can be used for a lighter texture.

Norwich Creamed Veal Kidneys

One of the most beautiful sights as you approach Norwich is the magnificent Cathedral, and not far away is Bridewell Alley, the home of Colman's Mustard Shop. It is said that this recipe was one of the very first to be served to Horatio Nelson, who attended King Edward VI School in the Cathedral precincts.

75g/3oz butter
8 veal kidneys, trimmed and sliced thinly
175g/6oz button mushrooms, sliced
1 tsp Colman's mustard
pinch of freshly minced ginger
salt and freshly ground black pepper

2 tbsp dry sherry
150ml/¼pt double cream

Garnish
4 slices of hot toast, cut into triangles
sprigs of fresh parsley

- Pre-heat the oven to 190°C/375°F/gas mark 5.
- Melt the butter in a large saucepan and gently fry the kidneys for 4 minutes. Remove the kidneys with a slotted spoon into a serving dish and keep warm.
- Add the mushrooms to the frying pan, cooking them in the left-over juices. Add the mustard, ginger, salt and freshly ground black pepper. Cook for 2 minutes, then add the sherry and cream. Cook for a further 3 minutes, then pour over the kidneys. Bake in the oven for 10 minutes.
- Place triangles of warm toast around the kidneys, garnish with sprigs of fresh parsley and serve.

FISH AND SEAFOOD

Medley of Seafood on a Bed of Rose Petal Cream Sauce

Fresh Sea Bass

English Kedgeree

Somerset Fish Casserole

Trout with Smoked Bacon

Baked Tanrogans

Seafood Crumble

Sewin with Leek and Orange

Poached Salmon with a Lemon and Watercress Sauce

Fresh Haddock with Potato Topping and Parsley Sauce

North Staffordshire Swallows

Salmon and Trout Fish Cakes

Fish 'n' Chips

I believe that fish and chips first saw light on the Yorkshire and Lancashire borders, although the seafood bars started in Brighton. Colchester opened the oyster bar, and eel and mash is without doubt a London delicacy. You will find some of my recipes very healthy and quite modern, but I am sure you will recognize other traditional dishes from around the coast of Britain. I started my mini-tour of Britain in London, where I visited Bentley's Seafood Restaurant with the oldest swinger in town, Tom Langley. Bentley's at Piccadilly, with oysters galore, buckets of mussels and every fish imaginable, was established in 1916, and today it has everything from plaice and chips to every taste of Britain on the menu.

Medley of Seafood served with a Vegetable Mousse

Medley of Seafood
ON A BED OF ROSE PETAL CREAM SAUCE

You can use almost any sea fish in this recipe, but I particularly like red sea bream. Use either tiger prawns or lobster tails. The photograph on page 38 shows a variation on this recipe of lobster tail on a vegetable mousse, garnished with a lemon basket and cucumber leaves. The choice is yours!

450g/1lb fillet of bream
12 crevettes
50g/2oz butter
12 scallops
12 tiger prawns
125g/4oz freshwater prawns
freshly ground black pepper
juice and zest of 1 lemon
saffron (powder or strands)

Sauce
150ml/¼pt rose petal vinegar
pink peppercorns
150ml/¼pt good quality white wine

6 turned carrots
salt and freshly ground black pepper
150ml/¼pt double cream or fromage frais

Vegetable stock
1 carrot, diced
1 onion, diced
1 stick of celery, diced
1 leek, chopped
1 bay leaf
bouquet garni
1 tbsp fresh herbs
1 clove of garlic, chopped

• Prepare the stock by placing the vegetables in 1l/1¾pt water, with the bay leaf, bouquet garni, herbs and garlic. Simmer for 1 hour, strain and place to one side.
• Fillet the sea bream, slice into cuts and place to one side. Place the crevettes on their side and cut down the spine with a sharp knife.
• Melt the butter in a large saucepan and add all the fish. Cook for 1–2 minutes, season with ground black pepper. Add 1 tbsp of lemon juice and the lemon zest.
• Very carefully add a pinch of saffron powder or a few strands to the juice and butter in the pan (not over the fish). Remove the pan from the heat and place the seafood in layers on a warm plate. Put the plate in the oven to keep warm.
• Return the pan with the juices to the heat, add the vegetable stock, bring to the boil and reduce by one-third.
• Add the rose petal vinegar and let it reduce for 4 minutes. Add the peppercorns, the rest of the lemon juice, the white wine and turned carrots, season, then allow the sauce to reduce for a further 6 minutes.
• Pour over the cream and simmer for 2 minutes.
• Remove the fish from the oven and lightly mask the fish with the sauce, placing the carrots around the plate.
• If you are serving this as a main course, mash the vegetables left from the stock with some potatoes and make them into little patty shapes, coat in egg and bread-crumbs and shallow fry them in a little melted butter or cooking oil.

Fresh Sea Bass

This is one of my favourite recipes, and I created it for a famous British fish company. As we head into the new millennium I think we are going to see a great deal more of this style of food, using more spices and herbs. The fish itself is not cooked.

8 x 100g/4oz medallions, filleted, skin and
  bones removed

Sauce
4 shallots, peeled and chopped
25g/1oz low-fat butter
10 cardamom pods
2 star anise

1 tbsp coriander seeds, crushed
trimmings from fresh ginger
black pepper
300ml/½pt white wine
300ml/½pt fish stock
300ml/½pt double cream or fromage frais
salt and freshly ground black pepper
juice of 1 lemon

- Cook the shallots in the butter for 4 minutes, add the spices and cook for a further 3 minutes.
- Add the wine and fish stock, reduce by half, add the cream, reduce again by half. Season well with salt and freshly ground black pepper, finish with the lemon juice.
- Pour the sauce over the medallions and garnish with fresh slices of lemon and shredded leek and carrot.

English Kedgeree

Known as 'kitchri' and originally a spicy Indian recipe containing onions and lentils, the recipe was brought back to Britain as a breakfast dish in the eighteenth century by the nabobs of the East India Company.

450g/1lb cooked finnan haddock, bone and
  skin removed
50g/2oz best butter
saffron powder
175g/6oz cooked long-grain rice
3 eggs, hard boiled and shelled

2 tbsp double cream
salt and freshly ground black pepper

Garnish
freshly chopped parsley
coriander leaves

- Flake the cooked finnan haddock, making sure all the bones and skin are removed.
- Melt the butter in a medium sized saucepan, add the fish with a pinch of saffron. Chop the eggs and add them with the rice to the saucepan.
- Gently heat all the ingredients together, slowly add the cream, stirring thoroughly, season with salt and freshly ground black pepper and serve hot with a sprinkle of freshly chopped parsley or coriander leaves.

Somerset Fish Casserole

Somerset is one of the most picturesque places in Europe, and I have friends from every corner of Britain who enjoy visiting this part of the country not just for their favourite cider but also for the cross-border day trips to the Cornish Riviera to taste Stargazy Pie or to visit Cheddar Gorge to see the mature cheese being made. Here is a taste of Somerset without the hassle of traffic jams or a train strike.

450g/1lb brill fillets, skinned and chopped
450g/1lb hake fillets, skinned and chopped
75g/3oz plain flour
salt and freshly ground black pepper
75g/3oz best butter
4 shallots, skinned and finely chopped
1 carrot, peeled and diced
1 leek, washed and finely chopped

300ml/½ pt Somerset dry cider
300ml/½ pt rough, medium-sweet, scrumpy
  cider
2 tsp anchovy essence
1 tbsp tarragon vinegar

Garnish
chopped fresh parsley

• Coat the fish in 25g/1oz of the seasoned flour. Melt the butter in a heatproof casserole and add the fish, shallots, carrot and leeks, cooking gently for 10 minutes. Sprinkle with the remaining flour, stirring for 2 minutes.
• Slowly add the ciders, anchovy essence and tarragon vinegar. Bring to the boil and simmer for 35 minutes on a low heat or bake in the oven for 30 minutes at 180°C/350°F/gas mark 4.
• Sprinkle with freshly chopped parsley and serve with warm crusty brown bread.

Trout with Smoked Bacon

This is an excellent barbecue recipe, but it is based on the traditional cooking method that has been used for thousands of years. I love bacon, too, and we have some of the finest curers on our doorstep. There is no need to go abroad. British bacon is not injected with water, and our curers produce the finest smoked bacon in Europe, so, please, always ask for British!

4 x 275g/10oz trout, gutted and cleaned
salt and freshly ground black pepper
2 apples, peeled, cored and sliced
4 sprigs of mint
juice of 1 lemon
12 rashers smoked streaky bacon, rindless

25g/1oz butter

Garnish
2 apples, cored and sliced
4 sprigs of freshly washed mint

• Pre-heat the oven to 200°C/400°F/gas mark 6.
• Open up the cavities of each trout and wash through thoroughly with warm salted water. Season each cavity with salt and freshly ground black pepper, place equal amounts of sliced apple in each cavity and add a sprig of mint. Squeeze over lemon juice.
• Carefully cover the whole of the trout in spirals of bacon, except the heads and tails.
• Grease a deep baking tray with the butter and place the trout, with the loose ends of bacon underneath, on the tray. Season with freshly ground black pepper and bake for 20 minutes, turning the trout after 10 minutes.
• Remove them from the oven onto a serving dish, garnish with sliced apple and fresh mint.

Baked Tanrogans

This is another dish that originated from the Isle of Man, where the word 'tanrogan' means scallop shell.

12 scallops	freshly ground black pepper
150ml/¼pt fish stock	juice of 2 lemons and zest
1 onion, chopped	150ml/¼pt double cream
salt	200g/8oz grated Cheddar cheese

- Pre-heat the oven to 180°C/350°F/gas mark 4.
- Remove the scallops from their shells. Scrape off the surrounding fringe (beard) and the black intestinal thread. The white part is the flesh and the orange part (coral) is the roe. Very carefully ease the flesh and coral from the shell with a short but very strong knife. Wash the shells thoroughly and dry them.
- Place all 12 shells on a baking sheet and place to one side.
- Put the scallops, fish stock, onion, salt and freshly ground black pepper in an ovenproof baking dish. Cover with cooking foil and bake for 8 minutes.
- Remove the foil and, with a slotted spoon, replace the scallops in their shells. Add 1 tbsp of the fish stock liquid to each shell, with a squeeze of lemon, a little double cream and grated cheese to top each shell.
- Return the scallops to the oven for a further 4 minutes, turning up the temperature to 230°C/450°/gas mark 8.
- Serve the scallops on their own with crusty brown bread and butter.

Seafood Crumble

Seafood Crumble is one of those dishes in which you can use any fish and any sauce you like. The ingredients vary widely across the country – in Devon they use a cider sauce, in Scotland they add smoked finnan haddock with a little whisky sauce, around Whitby in Yorkshire they use cheese sauce with cod. Every recipe seems to include prawns, but I like the Welsh method, which uses a leek sauce with honey and cheese.

450g/1lb smoked finnan haddock, filleted, skin removed and flaked	50g/2oz plain flour
100g/4oz prawns	600ml/1pt warm milk
100g/4oz sole fillet, skin removed and sliced	2 tbsp honey
freshly ground black pepper	75g/3oz Caerphilly cheese, grated
juice of 1 lemon	
	Crumble
Sauce	50g/2oz butter, softened
50g/2oz butter	75g/3oz flour
3 leeks, cleaned and very thinly sliced	75g/3oz Cheddar cheese, grated
	salt and freshly ground black pepper

100g/4oz butter
450g/1lb fresh haddock fillet, cut into 4 slices
600ml/1 pint milk
25g/1oz plain flour
freshly ground black pepper

pinch of freshly grated nutmeg
4 tbsp double cream
3 tbsp freshly chopped parsley
450g/1lb potatoes, boiled and mashed
100g/4oz finely shredded cabbage

- Pre-heat the oven to 200°C/400°F/gas mark 6. Use 25g/1oz of the butter to grease an ovenproof dish.
- Place the haddock fillets in the dish, pour over the milk and bake for 15 minutes. Remove from the oven and carefully pour the milk into a jug, being very careful not to break the fish.
- Melt the remaining butter in a saucepan and stir in the flour. Slowly whisk in the milk in which the fish was cooked and season with the pepper and nutmeg.
- Stirring all the time, add 3 tbsp cream and 2 tbsp parsley and cook for 2 minutes. Blend thoroughly and keep warm.
- Remove from the heat and add the remaining cream and parsley to the mashed potato. Pipe over the top of the haddock and return the dish to the oven for 6 minutes. Deep fry the shredded cabbage until crisp. Place the haddock in the centre of a plate, pour the sauce over the haddock and garnish with cabbage.

North Staffordshire Swallows

This sandwich-style fish recipe comes from the Potteries, home of hot oatcakes and the finest crockery in Britain. The idea is brilliant – it's like having fish and chips without the chips! A good beer batter with saffron and corn oil is the only way this recipe should be made. If you are on a diet, make it for your family and friends and serve it with lots of salt and malt vinegar.

450g/1lb cod fillet, skin removed
4 large potatoes, peeled and sliced to
   3mm/⅛in thick
salt and freshly ground black pepper
cocktail sticks

Batter
100g/4oz plain flour

pinch of salt
2 eggs
275ml/½pt milk
2 tbsp beer
1 tbsp oil
pinch of saffron

550g/1lb dripping

• Slice the uncooked cod slightly smaller than the size of the sliced potato, so that they will fit like a sandwich. Place a slice of fish on a slice of potato, season well and cover with another slice of potato. Hold together with a cocktail stick.
• Heat the dripping in a large deep frying pan.
• Mix the batter ingredients (see page 49).
• Dip the cod sandwiches into the beer batter and fry for at least 5–6 minutes until golden-brown, place them on some paper kitchen towel to drain.
• Season with salt and vinegar and serve with mushy peas, bread and butter.

Salmon and Trout Fish Cakes

Over the last 400 years the fish cake has packed its bag and moved from the coastlines around Britain from household to household. Then one day, a chef by the name of Tom Bridge decided it was time we changed some of the recipe. But only the recipe not the size – a fish cake should look like a fish cake and not be the size of a 50 pence piece. These fish cakes, which should be served with parsley sauce, are not available in supermarkets, so with this in mind I asked Steve Johnstone at Dalhousie Castle in Edinburgh if we could re-create this recipe using the finest Scottish ingredients.

450g/1lb fresh salmon fillet, skin removed and any excess bones
450g/1lb fresh trout fillet, skin removed and any excess bones
3 eggs, beaten
450g/1lb cooked potato mashed

175g/6oz breadcrumbs
50ml/2fl oz double cream
salt and freshly ground black pepper
1 tbsp parsley, freshly chopped

corn oil

• Flake the raw fish and add it to the rest of the ingredients, blending them thoroughly in a mixer or blender or by hand.

• Shape the mixture into fish cake shapes about 3cm/1¼ in thick and about 7cm/3in wide. Place the fish cakes in hot corn oil and fry for 4–5 minutes until golden-brown on both sides. Drain them on kitchen paper.

Fish 'n' Chips

How could I possibly finish the fish section without a recipe for fish and chips? This is the recipe my mother used when we were living in Hill Street in Bolton, Lancashire. I was ten years old and in love with Jaqueline Appleyard. I often wonder what happened to that very pretty girl. This wonderful recipe has its roots in Scarborough, Whitby and Bridlington, where the haddock and cod are caught that go into every fish and chip shop in every town and every village across Yorkshire and Lancashire.

corn oil or sunflower cooking oil
4 x 225g/8oz cod fillets
approximately 1kg/2lb potatoes, peeled and chipped
salt and freshly ground white pepper

Batter
200g/7oz plain flour
1 egg whisked with 2 tbsp beer
150ml/¼pt milk and water mixed
salt and freshly ground white pepper

• To make the batter mix the flour, egg, milk and seasoning, whisking until the mixture is very smooth and lump free. Leave it to stand for at least 1 hour.

• Heat the oil until it gives off a faint, almost invisible blue smoke (180°C/350°F). Fry the chips in small batches. When they start to brown remove them with a small slotted spoon or, if you use a basket, the basket. Place them in a warm oven.

• Season each piece of fish, then dip into the batter, drawing it backwards and forwards 2–3 times so that the fish is completely coated. Then lower each fish gently into the hot fat, with skin side down to prevent the fish from curling.

• Fry the fish one at a time. After 5 minutes, turn the fish over, and cook for a further 3 minutes until golden-brown.

• Traditionally, the fish and chips should be served on newspaper with salt and malt vinegar.

MEAT

Roast Saddle of Lakeland Lamb with Apricot Stuffing

*Lancashire Sirloin of English Beef Roasted with a Herb Crust and a Mustard
Seed Yorkshire Pudding*

Roast Loin of English Pork

Shrewsbury Lamb Cutlets

Crown of Welsh Lamb

Chesterfield Veal

Victorian Pot Roast Beef

Mutton Stew and Norfolk Dumplings

Lamb Cutlets Reform

Lobscouse

Lancashire Hotpot

Northern Irish Coddle

Braised Steak and Onions in a Whisky Sauce

Homemade Sausages

Beef Olives

Braised Shank of Warwickshire Lamb with Horseradish Dumplings

Euan Rodger's Roast Hovingham Lamb Henry

Lowestoft Corned Beef Hash

A Very W.I.S.E. Recipe

Norfolk Farmhouse Grill

'I learnt to think that it was not a stupid thing to cook'
Rosa Lewis, The Cavendish Hotel, 81 Jermyn Street, London, 1885

Roast Saddle of Lakeland Lamb with Apricot Stuffing

Roast Saddle of Lakeland Lamb with Apricot Stuffing

There are not many hotels in this country that can boast that they breed their own Herdwick sheep for their restaurants. Carol Fletcher spends hours on the Lakeland hills tending her sheep, and they really are well and truly looked after. The Nanny Brow Country House Hotel near Ambleside, Cumbria, asked me to create a signature dish for their restaurant using their home-bred lamb, and this recipe is similar to the one I devised for them. The original version is accompanied with two sauces, one a clear mint and orange and the other a grain mustard, and is garnished with rounds of minced lamb around black pudding. Serve this with Bubble and Squeak Vegetable-filled Cakes (see page 98). You can use shoulder or leg of lamb, boned and rolled, instead of saddle if you prefer.

1.8kg/4lb saddle of lamb, boned
salt and freshly ground black pepper
100g/4oz spinach

Stuffing
225g/8oz dried apricots, soaked overnight in
  orange juice

1 large onion, finely chopped
100g/4oz breadcrumbs
1 tsp dried mint
1 egg, beaten

300ml/10fl oz lamb stock
150ml/5fl oz port

SERVES 6–8

- Pre-heat the oven to 200°/400°F/gas mark 6.
- Flatten the lamb and season all over with salt and freshly ground black pepper.
- Blanch the whole spinach leaves for 1 minute in boiling salted water, remove and wash under cold water, taking care not to break the leaves. Carefully remove the stalks and discard. Arrange half the leaves so that they cover the inside of the lamb.
- Remove the apricots from the juice and chop them roughly, reserving the juice for the sauce. Place the apricots, onion, breadcrumbs, mint and beaten egg in a bowl and blend them thoroughly. Season and evenly place the mixture on the spinach to cover the base of the lamb. Cover with the remaining spinach and roll up the saddle very tightly like a Swiss roll, securing it with string.
- Place the lamb in a deep baking tray, lightly oil and season, cover with cooking foil and bake for 90 minutes. Remove the foil and return to the oven for a further 15 minutes.
- Meanwhile, put the lamb stock into a saucepan with the left-over orange juice and port, bring to the boil, reduce by half and leave until the lamb is cooked. Place the meat on a large serving plate and allow it to cool slightly. Add any juices from the roasting tin to the sauce, strain into a gravy boat and serve.

Lancashire Sirloin of English Beef

ROASTED WITH A HERB CRUST AND A MUSTARD SEED YORKSHIRE PUDDING

When Sir Richard Hoghton invited King James I to have a little lunch at Hoghton Tower near Preston he could never have known that a new word was to be added to the culinary dictionary. Brought to the table on that day of festivities was a magnificent loin of beef, which so delighted the king that he knighted it there and then, saying: 'Arise Sir Loin of Beef.' To honour these festivities, chef-proprietor Barry Rea, who runs the well-known Coppull Moor Restaurant, and I created this especially for you.

1.4kg/3lb sirloin of beef
100g/4oz dripping, melted
75g/3oz breadcrumbs
2 tsp mixed herbs
pinch of Madras curry powder

Yorkshire pudding batter (see page 24)
2 tbsp mustard seed
dripping

- Pre-heat the oven to 180°C/350°F/gas mark 4.
- Trim the excess fat from the beef and cut in a little pocket. Place the beef in a shallow baking tin on half of the melted dripping.
- Mix the breadcrumbs, herbs and curry powder in a bowl to make a paste and cover the top of the sirloin, then roast in the oven for 70 minutes.
- Increase the oven temperature to 220°C/425°F/gas mark 7, put the rest of the dripping in a large baking tray and place in the oven for 3 minutes until the dripping is smoking. Pour in the Yorkshire pudding batter into which the mustard seeds have been whisked and bake for 30 minutes.
- Remove both the meat and Yorkshire pudding. Carve the beef, make a gravy with the beef juices and serve with the mustard seed Yorkshire pudding.

Roast Loin of English Pork

To make perfect crackling, you must score it evenly. Penetrate the skin and a little of the fat below it with a very sharp knife, making diamond-shaped cuts about 1cm/½in long. Gently brush the pork generously with a little oil and salt.

1–3kg/2–6lb loin of pork
coarse salt and freshly ground black pepper
fresh rosemary

bay leaves
honey
2 pears, poached and quartered

SERVES 4–6

- Pre-heat the oven to 230°C/450°F/gas mark 8.
- To get the crackling really crisp, place the joint skin side down in a roasting tray and pour in about 2.5cm/1in of boiling water. Place the tray into the centre of the oven and cook for 20 minutes. Remove the tray, pour off the liquid and use it for basting the pork.
- Place the pork back into the roasting tray skin side up, season and insert a few bay leaves and rosemary needles into the score marks.
- Reduce the heat to 180°C/350°F/gas mark 4. Cook for 30 minutes per 450g/1lb, basting every 20 minutes. Allow the meat to cool.
- Remove the crackling, cut it into long thin strips, place it on a baking tray, salt and coat with a little honey. Add the pears and cook for a further 10 minutes.
- Arrange the slices of pork and crackling in a fanned circle and serve, hot or cold, accompanied by pickled red cabbage with cinnamon sticks and garnished with fresh thyme, if liked.

Carol tending her sheep

Shrewsbury Lamb Cutlets

25g/1oz butter
8 x 100g/4oz loin of lamb cutlets, trimmed
100g/4oz button mushrooms, sliced
100g/4oz shallots, peeled and sliced
4 tbsp redcurrant jelly
1 tsp Worcestershire sauce
juice of 1 lemon
25g/1oz plain flour

300ml/½pt meat stock
sprig of mint, finely chopped
pinch of nutmeg
salt and freshly ground black pepper

Garnish
sprig of mint
bunch of red berries

• Pre-heat the oven to 170°C/325°F/gas mark 3.
• Melt the butter in a frying pan and brown the cutlets on both sides, cooking for about 4 minutes. Place the cutlets in a large casserole with the mushrooms and shallots. Add the redcurrant jelly, Worcestershire sauce and lemon juice to the frying pan. Add the flour and blend thoroughly to make a smooth paste and cook for 3 minutes.
• Slowly add the stock and cook for 10 minutes. Add the mint and nutmeg and season well. Pour the sauce over the cutlets and cook in the centre of the oven for 90 minutes.
• Garnish the casserole with a sprig of fresh mint and the red berries, and serve with fresh oatcakes.

Crown of Welsh Lamb

Lamb is undoubtedly one of the most popular cuts of meat in the British cookery calendar. Once a month, I treat myself in different restaurants, trying different versions of this classic dish. This is, I think, one of the better of the modern recipes.

2 best end necks of lamb, with 6 cutlets, chinned on each
1 tbsp butter
1 onion, finely chopped
1 tsp rosemary, freshly ground
1 eating apple, cored and chopped
1 pear, cored and chopped
100g/4oz fresh breadcrumbs

2 tbsp mint, freshly chopped
1 egg
salt and freshly ground black pepper
3 tbsp clear honey

Garnish
4 x 100g/4oz slices of black pudding

- Pre-heat the oven to 180°C/350°F/gas mark 4.
- Trim each cutlet bone to a depth of 2.5cm/1in with a sharp knife. Bend the joints around, fat side inwards, to form a crown. Cover each exposed bone with cooking foil and place the meat in a small baking tray.
- Slowly melt the butter in a saucepan, add the onion, rosemary, apple and pear and cook for 4 minutes. Add the breadcrumbs, mint and egg. Season well.
- Fill the centre of the crown with the stuffing. Cover the crown with cooking foil and bake for 80 minutes.
- About 10 minutes before the end of cooking time, remove the foil and pour the honey around the sides of the crown, making sure it does not touch the top of the crown. Replace the foil and return to the oven.
- Grill the black pudding for 3 minutes each side. Serve the lamb garnished with slices of black pudding and accompanied by fresh shallots glazed with the honey juices from the lamb and baked parsnip with mint and onion gravy.

Chesterfield Veal

Chesterfield used to be famous for its veal, and in the eighteenth century one of the most famous recipes in the Midlands was Love in Disguise, which was calf's heart filled with a veal forcemeat, coated in breadcrumbs and baked in the oven. Following is quite a simple nineteenth-century recipe, which could possibly have been served during a hunt supper. If you prefer not to serve veal, pork cutlets are a good alternative.

75g/3oz butter
4 x 250g/9oz veal cutlets, trimmed
1 large onion, sliced
2 apples, peeled, cored and sliced
175g/6oz button mushrooms
1 tbsp coriander leaves, chopped
8 black peppercorns

1 tbsp sesame seeds
2 large tomatoes, cut in half
salt and freshly ground black pepper

Garnish
coriander leaves

- Pre-heat the oven to 150°C/300°F/gas mark 2.
- Melt 50g/2oz of the butter in a large frying pan and gently fry the cutlets for 5 minutes on each side. Remove the cutlets from the pan, place them on a dish and keep them warm in the oven.
- In the same frying pan, fry the onions and apple slices together, browning the apple slightly.
- Place the apple and onions in a serving dish, arrange the cutlets, placing them on the onion and apple slices, and keep them warm in the oven.
- In the same frying pan, melt the remaining butter and gently fry the mushrooms, coriander and peppercorns. Cook for 3 minutes then sprinkle the sesame seeds over the mushrooms.
- Place the mushroom, peppercorns and juices on the cutlets, place the tomatoes around the edge of the cutlets and return to the oven for a further 5 minutes.
- Season well with salt and freshly ground black pepper, and garnish with coriander leaves before serving.

Victorian Pot Roast Beef

This very ancient dish has been copied by almost every cook and chef. In 1862 Queen Victoria's chef, Charles Elmé Francatelli, claimed it was his own recipe, and he called it 'Braised Beef à la Polonaise aux Choux Rouges'. I have modernized the recipe a little, but the flavours and method are still Victorian, and it is a regular feature on my dinner table.

1.4kg/3lb topside of beef
50g/2oz butter
20 shallots, peeled
4 large potatoes, peeled and quartered
2 large carrots, peeled and cut into chunks
2 parsnips, peeled and cut into chunks
1 small turnip, peeled and chopped
sprig of fresh thyme
sprig of rosemary

salt
freshly ground black pepper
300ml/½pt beef stock
150ml/¼pt of good quality red wine
2 tbsp cornflour blended with a little red wine

Garnish
sprigs of thyme

- Pre-heat the oven to 200°C/400°F/gas mark 6.
- Quickly fry the topside of beef in the butter, browning the beef well all over, then place it to one side.
- Fry the shallots, potatoes, carrot, parsnip and turnip in the butter and beef juice, then place the beef, surrounded by the vegetables, in a large, deep casserole or pot. Add all the remaining ingredients, except the cornflour.
- Cover with a lid or cooking foil and place in the centre of the oven and cook for 2 hours. After 90 minutes, remove the lid or foil to allow the meat to brown a little more.
- Carefully place the meat and vegetables on a large serving dish and remove the thyme and rosemary sprigs. Bring the stock juices to the boil and add the cornflour blended with a little wine. Cook and simmer for 4 minutes and pour around the vegetables. Serve garnished with fresh thyme.

Lobscouse

This recipe is dedicated to my Auntie Doreen. I have relatives all over Liverpool and they have to be the friendliest, most humorous and warmest people, I have ever met. This recipe was given to me by my father-in-law, Jim Fitzpatrick, who still lives in Bootle. The recipes for Lobscouse vary all over the country – some use silverside, some add peas, and some add swede. This is the best and tastiest recipe I have ever come across, and my wife Jayne, who is a Liverpool Belle, swears that it is the original!

50g/2oz dripping
900g/2lb neck of lamb, fat removed and cut
   into cubes, soaked in 600ml/1pt meat stock
   overnight
450g/1lb stewing steak, fat removed and cubed

3 large onions, peeled and sliced
900g/2lb potatoes, peeled and sliced
2 carrots, peeled and sliced
salt and freshly ground black pepper

• Pre-heat the oven to 170°C/325°F/gas mark 3 and melt the dripping in a deep ovenproof casserole.
• Remove the lamb from the stock and dry it in some paper kitchen towel. Seal the lamb and steak by frying quickly in the hot dripping, add the onions and cook for 6 minutes.
• 'Lob' all the ingredients into the casserole, add the beef stock and just enough water to just cover the ingredients. Cover the casserole with a lid or cooking foil and cook in the centre of the oven for 4 hours until the scouse is completely cooked and blended together.

> For Blind Scouse add an extra assortment of vegetables, totalling about 900g/2lb, and omit the meat.

Lancashire Hotpot

❋

MANCHESTER is noted for its hotpots and has a special one of its own, but the following excellent recipe comes from Bolton-le-Moors ('Bowton'). The oysters may be omitted, but they are the correct thing in a real hotpot.

Another correct thing is to serve Lancashire hotpot with a dish or glass jar of pickled red cabbage whatever recipe be used. This is traditional.

Florence White, *Good Things in England*, 1932

❋

This is my revised version of the traditional recipe.

50g/2oz dripping
900g/2lb middle neck of mutton, trimmed
 and cut into chops
2 large onions, peeled and sliced
25g/1oz plain flour
600ml/1pt meat stock

salt and freshly ground black pepper
100g/4oz lambs kidney, diced
225g/8oz button mushrooms
10 oysters, washed and beard removed
 (optional)
900g/2lb potatoes, peeled and thinly sliced

- Pre-heat the oven to 190°C/375°F/gas mark 5.
- Heat the dripping in a large frying pan and quickly brown the chops, cooking for about 3 minutes. Remove the chops to a large ovenproof casserole with a lid and keep them warm in a low oven.
- Fry the onions for about 3 minutes, until they become transparent, add the flour and cook for 2 minutes. Slowly add the stock and season well, stirring all the time.
- Remove the chops from the oven and place the kidneys, mushrooms and oysters with the chops, interlayering them with the potatoes. Pour over the onion stock and cook in the centre of the oven for 2 hours. Take off the lid for the last 15 minutes to brown the potatoes.

Northern Irish Coddle

For well over 100 years McCartney's family butchers of Moira, County Down, have been supplying award-winning sausages to their customers from around the world, including myself. With over thirty-five varieties available, you will find it very hard to decide which kind to use in the Coddle.

50g/2oz lard or dripping
450g/1lb Irish sausage
175g/6oz Irish back bacon, rindless and
 chopped
175g/6oz lamb's kidney, chopped
2 large onions, peeled and sliced

25g/1oz plain flour
600ml/1pt chicken stock
150ml/¼pt Guinness
900g/2lb potatoes, peeled and chopped
salt
freshly ground black pepper

- Heat the lard or dripping in a large saucepan and gently fry the sausage, bacon, kidney and onions for 6 minutes. Add the flour and cook for 1 minute. Slowly add the chicken stock and Guinness, stirring constantly.
- Add the potatoes and season well. Simmer on a low heat for 90 minutes, stirring every 15 minutes. Serve with Irish soda bread and a pint of Guinness.

Braised Steak and Onions in a Whisky Sauce

I often wonder whatever happened to chefs Alister McGovern and Tony Smith, to whom I taught this recipe while I was working in Burns's country, Ayr. The sauce is thickened with thin slices of haggis, before being strained and served with warm beetroot and the braised steak and onions. I devised the recipe for Burns's Night in 1973, basing it on a recipe from the 1840s.

25g/1oz cooking oil
50g/2oz flour, seasoned
4 x 225g/8oz braising steak, fat and gristle
  removed
450g/1lb baby onions or shallots (peeled
  weight), sliced

175g/6oz haggis, thinly sliced
150ml/¼pt meat stock
100ml/2fl oz whisky
1 tsp Worcestershire sauce
salt and freshly ground black pepper

- Pre-heat the oven to 150°C/300°F/gas mark 2.
- Heat the oil in a large frying pan. Coat the steaks in the seasoned flour and brown them on both sides, cooking for about 3 minutes each side. Place them in a large deep casserole and sprinkle with the sliced onions.
- Slowly fry the haggis in the steak juices, breaking it up slowly. Add the stock and whisky and cook for 10 minutes. Add the Worcestershire sauce and taste, then season with the salt and freshly ground black pepper.
- Strain the sauce through a fine sieve over the steak and onions. Cover the casserole with a lid or cooking foil and place in the centre of the oven. Cook for 2 hours until the meat is very tender and serve with warm baby beetroot and good chunky chips.

Homemade Sausages

You can buy sausage machines at many good cookware stores, and your butcher will also sell sausage skins. I think the flavour of homemade sausages is always better than the shop-bought variety. If you have a large piping bag with a wide nozzle, simply put the skins on the end of the nozzle and squeeze the sausage mixture into them. The method is quite simple – you just mix the ingredients together in a large bowl.

900g/2lb very lean pork, roughly minced
  (your butcher will do this for you)
350g/12oz shredded vegetable suet
1 large onion, peeled and very finely chopped
225g/8oz fresh white breadcrumbs, very fine

1 tsp salt
1 tsp freshly ground black pepper
1 tsp powdered sage
1 tsp parsley

• Blend all the ingredients together.
• Use either a machine or a piping bag with a wide nozzle and piping bag, knot one end of the skin and slowly pipe the mixture into the skin. When the skin is full, draw it away from the nozzle, knot the end and twist the skin at intervals of about 10cm/4in.
• Place the sausages in the fridge for at least 6 hours to allow the mixture to blend properly before using for sausage and mash, Toad in th'Hole or a good fry-up. Cook for 6–8 minutes all over until they are golden-brown.

Beef Olives

This is one of those recipes that originated in the Middle Ages and that has been transformed over the centuries. It started life as a filling for a full side of beef, veal, lamb or wild boar. Then it was transformed into escalopes of meat, fish and game because it was far easier to cook. You will need some butcher's string, strong thread or wooden cocktail sticks.

Stuffing
175g/6oz fine breadcrumbs
1 tbsp anchovy essence
4 tbsp finely chopped onion
2 tbsp ham, finely chopped
1 tsp parsley
1 tsp thyme
salt and freshly ground black pepper
1 egg beaten with 1 tbsp brandy

Olives and sauce
8 x 175g/6oz sirloin of beef escalopes
600ml/1pt beef stock
12 shallots, peeled
25g/1oz butter
25g/1oz flour
2 tbsp port
2 tbsp red wine
salt and freshly ground black pepper

- Pre-heat the oven to 180°C/350°F/gas mark 4.
- Place all the ingredients for the stuffing in a large mixing bowl and blend thoroughly for about 3 minutes. Roll the mixture into 8 large balls and place to one side.
- Flatten the steaks with a tenderizer or heavy rolling pin until they are very thin. Place a stuffing ball on the centre of each escalope and spread it flat. Roll the meat up into a Swiss roll shape and tie each parcel or olive with string or skewer with wooden cocktail sticks to hold in shape.
- Lay the olives in a lightly greased ovenproof casserole, add the stock and shallots, cover the dish and bake in the centre of the oven for 30 minutes.
- Carefully lift the beef olives from the casserole onto a warm serving dish, remove the string or cocktail sticks and surround with the shallots and keep warm.
- Melt the butter in a saucepan, add the flour and cook for 3 minutes, add the beef stock from the olives and bring to the boil. Let the sauce simmer then add the port and red wine, season and allow to simmer for 5 minutes.
- Pour the sauce over the beef olives and serve with new potatoes and crusty brown bread.

Braised Shank of Warwickshire Lamb

WITH HORSERADISH DUMPLINGS

This dish originates from the Hillfields area of Coventry. Traditionally, it was made with a cheap cut of meat, but today there is no such thing as cheap cut. For maximum flavour, make the dish 24 hours in advance.

4 x 225g/8oz shanks of lamb
450g/1lb onions, peeled and diced
2 large carrots, peeled and diced
100g/4oz swede, peeled and diced
150ml/¼pt brown ale
1 tsp tomato purée
600ml/1pt meat stock
salt and freshly ground black pepper
sprig of rosemary

Dumplings
225g/8oz plain flour, sifted
pinch of salt
100g/4oz vegetable suet
25g/1oz horseradish, freshly grated
6 tbsp water

- Pre-heat the oven to 200°C/400°F/gas mark 6.
- Place the shanks into a deep ovenproof casserole dish, and sprinkle over the vegetables.
- Put the brown ale, tomato purée, meat stock and seasoning in a bowl and blend thoroughly. Pour the liquid over the lamb and vegetables and add the sprig of rosemary. Cover with cooking foil and place in the centre of the oven and braise for 90 minutes.
- Meanwhile, make the dumplings by sifting the flour and salt into a clean bowl, add the suet and horseradish, blend and then sprinkle in the water. Stir with a fork to form a soft dough. Turn out the mixture on a floured board and divide the mixture into small ball shapes and set aside until the 90 minutes cooking time is up.
- Remove the foil, and give the lamb a good stir, turning each shank. Add the dumplings and return to the oven for a further 30 minutes. Serve on a large dish on a bed of mashed potato.

Euan Rodger's Roast Hovingham Lamb Henry

Hovingham is a picturesque place, with Hovingham Hall, the home of Sir Marcus Worsley, standing at the edge of the village. This recipe is a feature of the menu of the Worsley Arms, where chef Andrew Jones told me that a 'henry' is a cut from the shoulder of lamb with the blade bone left in. The dish takes three days to complete, but it is well worth it.

4 x 225g/8oz shoulder of lamb bone in
100g/4oz yellow split peas
200g/7oz yellow lentils
300ml/½pt chicken stock
1 bay leaf
1 tbsp warm honey
salt and freshly ground black pepper
200g/7oz mashed potato

Marinade
300ml/½pt lamb stock
2 tbsp warm honey
1 tbsp garlic, crushed
1 tsp peppercorns, crushed
1 tbsp Worcestershire sauce
1 tbsp dried rosemary

- Place the lamb in a deep casserole dish and cover with the marinade ingredients. Blend the ingredients and lamb together well and chill in the fridge for two days, blending the ingredients and the lamb together three times a day.
- Pre-heat the oven to 180°C/350°F/gas mark 4. Braise the lamb for 2 hours. Remove the lamb to a serving dish and keep warm. Pour the juices into a saucepan and bring to the boil rapidly. Reduce the liquid by half.
- Meanwhile, place the peas and lentils in a saucepan with the chicken stock and bay leaf, bring to the boil and simmer for 30 minutes. Add the honey and season well. Drain, remove the bay leaf and mash the peas, lentils and mashed potato together and place on the base of a plate.
- Place the lamb in the centre, and pour the sauce into a sauce boat. Garnish with sprigs of fresh rosemary and mashed potato.

Lowestoft Corned Beef Hash

This is one of those recipes you see in almost every café in Britain. I remember a winter's day in Lowestoft. I went into a little café near the station and ordered a cup of tea. All I could smell was fried onions, and I asked the waitress what they were cooking. She said it was going to be a corned beef hash for lunch, so I returned an hour later to enjoy a taste of tradition.

450g/1lb tin of corned beef
25g/1oz dripping
1 large onion, roughly chopped
1 tbsp mushroom ketchup
600ml/1pt meat stock, thickened with a little cornflour

900g/2lb cooked and mashed potatoes, buttered and seasoned
50g/2oz butter, melted
75g/3oz Cheddar cheese, grated
freshly ground black pepper

- Pre-heat the oven to 180°C/350°F/gas mark 4.
- Chop the cooked corned beef into 1cm/ ½ in cubes and place them in a casserole dish.
- Gently fry the onions in a little dripping, spread them over the corned beef cubes, sprinkle over the mushroom ketchup and cover with stock.
- Top with the mashed potato, melted butter and grated cheese and season with freshly ground black pepper. Bake for 20–25 minutes, until golden-brown.

A Very W.I.S.E. Recipe

This is another one of my slightly expensive creations, but it does serve 6–8 people and it is a really nice party piece. The meat must be sliced to look like small flat cakes. You could use fillet of Norfolk fillet or Lincolnshire duck breast instead of veal.

50g/2oz butter
50g/2oz sunflower oil
225g/8oz of the following meats, trimmed and cut into 50g/2oz pieces (rosettes):
   Welsh lamb fillet
   Irish pork fillet
   Scotch beef fillet
   English veal fillet
salt and freshly ground black pepper
225g/8oz leeks sliced
225g/8oz potato, cooked and sliced
100g/4oz haggis, cooked and sliced

100g/4oz black pudding, sliced
225g/8oz Savoy cabbage, very finely shredded, cooked
225g/8oz button mushrooms
25g/1oz plain flour
150ml/¼pt beef stock
4 tbsp double cream
2 tbsp Drambuie or whisky

Garnish
large bunch of watercress

- Pre-heat the oven to 150°C/300°F/gas mark 2.
- Melt the butter and oil in a large frying pan, fry each cut of meat for 4 minutes on each side and season well with salt and freshly ground black pepper. Place the meats on a large tray, remembering what each cut of meat is. Place in the oven to keep warm.
- Using the same pan, cook the leeks for 3 minutes and place to one side.
- Arrange the leeks, potato, haggis and black pudding around the edge of a large serving dish, leaving the centre of the dish empty. Place the slices of lamb on the leeks, the pork on the potato, the beef on the haggis, and the veal on the black pudding.
- Spread the cabbage over the centre of the dish and return to the oven for 12 minutes.
- Meanwhile, fry the mushrooms for 4 minutes in the same pan juices and fat, sprinkle with flour and cook for 2 minutes. Add the beef stock, cream and spirits, stirring continuously. Season with salt and freshly ground black pepper.
- Place the mushrooms and the sauce into the centre of the serving dish on the shredded cabbage. Garnish with fresh watercress and serve with nothing else.

Norfolk Farmhouse Grill

Norfolk really is farming country, and nowhere else in Britain will you find farmers tucking into a breakfast of this superb grill, which they wash down with a glass of cider.

salt and freshly ground black pepper
4 lamb cutlets, trimmed
4 pork sausages
4 x 175g/6oz rump steak
4 x 100g/4oz gammon steak
1 ring of black pudding cut into four, skin removed
2 lambs or pigs kidneys, cut into half

2 tbsp cooking oil
225g/8oz button mushrooms
2 large beef tomatoes

Garnish
fresh watercress
4 rings of pineapple or 4 poached eggs

• Season all the meats well with salt and freshly ground pepper, then grill all the meats until cooked for about 4 minutes each side. Grill or fry the black pudding for 3 minutes on each side. Place the meat on a large serving dish and keep hot in a warm oven.

• Add the cooking oil to a large frying pan and gently fry the mushrooms and tomatoes for 3 minutes.

• Place them around the meats, garnish with some watercress, and top the gammon steaks with a ring of fresh pineapple or a poached egg.

POULTRY AND GAME

Breast of Wild Lincolnshire Duckling with a Raspberry and Honey Sauce
Roast Grouse with Bacon and Dripping Triangles

Nelson's Breast of Chicken Cooked in Port and Lemon
with a Rum and Raisin Sauce

Braised Breast of Turkey with York Ham and Stilton Cheese
Garnished with Shallots and Baby Beetroot

Roast Goose with Mint, Onion and Orange Stuffing
Rosa's Quail Pudding
Pheasant with Baby Onions and Green Peas
Old English Game Sauce
Terrine of Pigeon and Black Pudding with a Rich Onion Marmalade
Roast Wood Pigeon in Cream
Rabbit with Rosemary and Cider Sauce
Venison Steak with Black Cherries
Beetroot and Rhubarb Chutney

We have an abundance of poultry and game of every possible kind in the British Isles, and I have personally tried and tasted every type of game bird that is native to Britain. The following selection includes some of my favourite dishes, which I devised for major food companies in the UK.

Breast of Duckling with a Raspberry and Honey Sauce

Breast of Wild Lincolnshire Duckling

WITH A RASPBERRY AND HONEY SAUCE

I wrote a similar recipe for my popular *Heartbeat Country Cookbook*, which was based on the popular Yorkshire Television series starring Nick Berry.

4 x 275g/10oz breast of duckling fillets, trimmed
salt and freshly ground black pepper
25g/1oz butter
50g/2oz carrots, finely chopped
100g/4oz whole shallots
1 tbsp lemon juice
150ml/¼pt meat stock

4 tbsp honey
100g/4oz fresh or frozen raspberries
25g/1oz flour
1 tsp Worcestershire sauce

Garnish
5 whole shallots

• Trim and score the duck breast and season well all over.
• Put the butter into the frying pan and seal the duck breasts. Add the carrots, shallots, lemon juice and a little of the stock. Let the sauce simmer for 1 minute, then add a little honey and a few raspberries and a sprinkle of flour. Allow it to cook for a few minutes, season with freshly ground black pepper and add the Worcestershire sauce.
• Then repeat the process, starting with the stock and honey, allowing 3 minutes for cooking time.
• Remove the duck breast from the pan, allowing the sauce to continue simmering. Slice the duck breast lengthways into 5mm/¼ in slices. Pour a little of the sauce onto the serving plate, arrange the duck breast into a fan shape and decorate with shredded and whole shallots.

Roast Grouse

WITH BACON AND DRIPPING TRIANGLES

Not so long ago, one in every five grand houses throughout Britain would have had this recipe served during the cold winter nights.

50g/2oz butter
juice of 1 lemon
225g/8oz redcurrants or cranberries
salt and freshly ground black pepper
4 oven-ready grouse

8 rashers streaky bacon
thyme
50g/2oz dripping
2 slices of bread cut into triangles

- Pre-heat the oven to 200°C/400°F/gas mark 6.
- Heat the butter in a saucepan and add the lemon juice and redcurrants or cranberries, with a sprinkle of salt and freshly ground black pepper. Cook for 1 minute and allow to cool.
- Fill the cavities of each bird with the redcurrants and juice, seasoning the birds all over with salt and freshly ground black pepper.
- Wrap 2 slices of streaky bacon over each breast. Sprinkle with thyme. Wrap each bird in some greased foil and place them, breast down, in a roasting tin. Roast for 15 minutes. Remove the foil and roast for a further 10 minutes.
- Heat the dripping in a frying pan and fry the bread triangles on both sides until golden-brown. Arrange the triangles on a large serving plate and place the grouse on the triangles to serve.

Nelson's Breast of Chicken

COOKED IN PORT AND LEMON WITH A RUM AND RAISIN SAUCE

This combination of foods was used on the tall ships, and it would have been served on Nelson's flagship HMS *Victory*. When the Tall Ships Race came to Liverpool, I devised this recipe as a tribute.

4 x 175g/6oz chicken breast fillet
50g/2oz butter
2 lemons, juice and zest
3 tbsp port
1 tbsp white wine

150g/5oz raisins
salt and freshly ground black pepper
4 tbsp dark rum
150ml/¼pt sour cream

- Cut the chicken fillets into thin slices, each weighing 25g/1oz and giving 6 per serving.
- Heat the butter in a frying pan, add the chicken and cook gently for 6 minutes, turning frequently until the meat is lightly coloured. Add the lemon and port and cook for a further 5 minutes. Remove from the pan and arrange in a spiral shape on a large serving plate. Keep warm.
- With the juices from the chicken in the pan, return the pan to the heat. Add the wine and raisins and simmer for 2 minutes. Season, add the dark rum and cook for a further 3 minutes. Finally add the cream and reduce by half. Pour the sauce into the centre of the chicken breast spiral and serve immediately with buttered asparagus.

Braised Breast of Turkey

WITH YORK HAM AND STILTON CHEESE
GARNISHED WITH SHALLOTS AND BABY BEETROOT

Beetroot seems to be doing a disappearing act from most British dining tables, but it will never disappear from mine. I really do think it is the most underrated of vegetables, adding flavour and colour to numerous dishes, including this one, which is another of my new recipes, devised especially for this book. It's for P.V. – keep trying!

450g/1lb Red Velvet Baby Beetroot
2 x 450g/1lb turkey breast
8 fresh sage leaves
salt and freshly ground black pepper
8 thin slices of York ham
225g/8oz Stilton cheese, sliced
225g/8oz streaky bacon, rindless
150ml/¼ pt chicken stock

2 tbsp port
24 shallots, peeled
1 large tbsp cornflour, blended with a little
  port

Garnish
8 sage leaves
8 seedless black grapes cut into halves

- Pre-heat the oven to 190°C/375°F/gas mark 5.
- To prepare the beetroot, cut off the leaf stalks about 2.5cm/1in above the root, but do not trim off the tapering bottom. Wash the beetroot carefully to prevent them from 'bleeding'. Steam or boil them in their skins for 1 hour in salted water. Allow them to cool naturally and remove the skins. Place them in a serving dish and keep warm.
- Cut a long horizontal slit along each turkey breast to make a pocket shape. Insert 4 sage leaves and lightly season. Wrap the ham around the cheese and place into the slits.
- Carefully wrap bacon around each breast, making sure that the pocket containing the cheese and ham is completely covered.

Andrew and the chefs at the Worsley Arms, Hovington, Yorkshire

- Place the turkey breasts in an ovenproof casserole dish, pour over the chicken stock and port, add the shallots, cover with a lid or cooking foil and braise for 40 minutes.
- Carefully place the turkey breasts on a cutting board and slice through them to make a fan effect. Put them on a warm serving dish with the shallots and beetroot.
- Put the juices from the casserole into a saucepan and bring to the boil, remove from the heat and add the cornflour paste, gently simmer and allow the sauce to cook gently for 2 minutes.
- Pour the sauce over the shallots and beetroot and garnish with some fresh sage leaves and sliced black grapes.

Roast Goose

WITH MINT, ONION AND ORANGE STUFFING

Goose is quite expensive today and I can afford to have this wonderful bird only on special occasions. But on a cold winter's day, dinner of roast goose, served with roast potatoes, fresh green buttered beans and giblet gravy is a meal to remember.

4.5kg/10lb goose, cleaned and trussed
3 tbsp orange juice
salt and freshly ground black pepper

Stuffing
50g/2oz butter
1 large onion, peeled and chopped
goose liver, finely chopped
175g/6oz Cumberland sausage meat
225g/8oz white breadcrumbs

1 tsp dried mint
225g/8oz orange segments, chopped
1 tsp finely chopped orange peel, soaked in
   1 tbsp orange liqueur
salt and freshly ground black pepper

Garnish
1 bunch watercress
1 orange, sliced
sprig of fresh mint

- Pre-heat the oven to 170°C/325°F/gas mark 3.
- Prick the goose all over with a fork, rub into the breast the orange juice and season well, including the cavity.
- Make the stuffing by melting the butter in a frying pan. Gently fry the onion and goose liver for 3 minutes, allow the mixture to cool and blend it with the rest of the ingredients in a clean bowl.
- Stuff the cavity of the goose with the mixture. Truss the goose and place it on a rack, placing the bird and rack into a roasting tray. A rack is needed so that the fat from the goose can drain away. The goose must be roasted slowly for 3 hours. For the first 30 minutes the goose should be breast side up, then turn it over onto its breast and cook for 1 hour, pouring the excess fat into a heat-resistant jug. Turn the goose back to breast side up and cook for the final 90 minutes. Test if the goose is cooked by inserting a metal meat skewer into the leg. If the juices run clear, it is cooked; if you see blood, cook for a further 20 minutes until the juices run clear.
- Place the goose onto a bed of watercress, garnished with slices of fresh orange and mint leaves. Allow the goose to cool slightly before carving.

Rosa's Quail Pudding

Rosa Lewis's life story was the inspiration for the classic television series *The Duchess of Duke Street*. Much of the script was based on her time as chef/proprietor of my favourite London hotel, the Cavendish in Jermyn Street (which is on the corner of Duke Street). She was famous for her game sauces and quail pudding, which she created for her long-time friend, Edward VII. Rosa also made her quail pudding for White's, one of London's longest established gentlemen's clubs, and she was advised by Auguste Escoffier, one of her regular clients. If you don't want to spend the time steaming the pudding, serve the quail meat sliced with vegetables and the sauce in a sauce boat. If you don't like quail meat, you can try this recipe with breast meat from your favourite game or with chicken breast. This recipe is dedicated to Joaquin (Jack) Rivas Casas, the Cavendish Hotel, London.

50g/2oz butter
pinch of fine herbs
8 quail breasts, skin removed
75g/3oz button mushrooms
50g/2oz shallots, sliced
150ml/¼pt fresh orange juice

sprig of fresh thyme
4 tbsp brandy
salt and freshly ground black pepper
150ml/¼pt game sauce (see page 77)
225g/8oz suet pastry (see page 92)

• Melt the butter in a large frying pan, add the herbs, quail breasts, mushrooms and shallots, and fry them for 6 minutes. Remove the breasts from the pan.
• Add the orange juice, thyme, brandy and seasoning to the pan and simmer for at least 20 minutes, until the liquid is reduced by half.
• Add the game sauce and simmer and reduce by half again. Place the quail meat and game sauce into a 20cm/8in pudding basin, which has been buttered and lined with suet pastry.
• Cover the top of the basin with suet pastry and seal. Gently brush the top with melted butter and cover with several layers of cooking foil. Steam the pudding in a covered saucepan for 2 hours, topping up the pan with extra water as necessary.
• Serve with fresh vegetables.

Pheasant
WITH BABY ONIONS AND GREEN PEAS

Mike Bevans, of the Linthwaite House Hotel at Bowness on Windermere, is very well known for his game recipes, and this favourite British dish is more than two centuries old.

225g/8oz pork fat, cut into small cubes
50g/2oz butter
16 small onions or shallots, peeled
2 large pheasants
25g/1oz plain flour

600ml/1pt chicken stock
bouquet garni
450g/1lb fresh peas
salt and freshly ground black pepper

- Pre-heat the oven to 200°C/400°F/gas mark 6.
- Place the pork fat cubes into a pan of boiling salted water and simmer for 3 minutes. Drain and dry.
- Melt the butter in a large frying pan, add the pork and onions, browning lightly for 3 minutes.
- Remove the pork and onions from the pan, add the pheasants and brown them all over. Remove them from the pan and place them on a baking tray.
- Add the flour to the pan and cook until it begins to brown, then slowly blend in the chicken stock.
- Cook the pheasants in the oven for 45 minutes with the sauce, seasoning and bouquet garni. Remove the bouquet garni 10 minutes before the end of cooking time and add the onions, pork, peas and seasoning.
- When cooked, place the pheasants on a large platter, surrounded with the pork, peas, onions and gravy.

Old English Game Sauce

When a game sauce is mentioned, everyone thinks of Cumberland Sauce. In fact, there are two categories of game – small game, such as hares, quail, partridge, pheasants, wild duck and so on, for which a Cumberland Sauce could be used, and venison, wild boar and so on, for which one would use a poivrade sauce.

2 tbsp McNeill's orange and green pepper
   vinegar
225g/8oz redcurrant jelly
2 tbsp port wine
1 blade of mace
1 small stick of cinnamon
1 bay leaf

lemon rind, finely chopped
2 shallots, finely chopped
pinch of salt
25g/1oz mushrooms, coarsely chopped
1 tbsp capers, finely chopped
4 black and 4 white peppercorns, freshly
   crushed

- Put the orange and green pepper vinegar, redcurrant jelly, port wine, mace, cinnamon, bay leaf, lemon rind and finely chopped shallots into a saucepan. Heat to boiling point, reduce the heat and simmer for 12 minutes. Add salt to taste.
- Strain into a sauce boat through a fine sieve, sprinkle with the mushrooms, capers and freshly ground peppercorns, blending them into the sauce before serving.

In 1783 John Farley published *The London Art of Cookery* in which he gave this recipe for Venison Sauce:

> Currant jelly warmed; or half pint of red wine, with a quarter of a pound of sugar, simmered over a clear fire for five or six minutes; or half a pint of vinegar, and a quarter pound of sugar, simmered till it be a syrup.

Terrine of Pigeon and Black Pudding

WITH A RICH ONION MARMALADE

This is another flavourful recipe from Cheshire,
and I include it with a thank you to Jeremy Rata.

450g/1lb boneless pigeon meat, roughly
  chopped
100ml/4fl oz brandy
225g/8oz minced pork
3 large onions, chopped
rind of 1 orange

salt and freshly ground black pepper
3 eggs, beaten
450g/1lb black pudding, diced
450g/1lb streaky bacon, rindless
25g/1oz butter
4 tbsp orange and whiskey marmalade

• Pre-heat the oven to 180°C/350°F/gas mark 4.
• Remove any fat or sinews from the pigeon meat, place it in a bowl with the brandy
and marinate for 3 hours. Add to this the pork and 3 tbsp of chopped onion, orange
rind, seasoning and the beaten eggs and blend the mixture thoroughly. Taking care
not to break the pieces, slowly blend the black pudding into the mixture.
• Line a 1.2l/2pt ovenproof terrine dish with slices of streaky bacon. Put in the
pigeon mixture, cover with the rest of the bacon, then with greased cooking foil.
Stand the terrine in a pan or baking tin and add hot water until it comes half way
up the sides of the terrine. Bake in the centre of the oven for 90 minutes. Remove
the foil and allow to cool naturally, then chill for at least 4 hours before serving.
• Fry the remaining onions gently for 2 minutes in the butter, add the marmalade
and cook for 3 minutes. Pour the onion marmalade onto individual plates and serve
with a generous slice of the terrine, garnished with slices of orange and fresh bread.

Roast Wood Pigeon in Cream

A delicacy since Roman times, this dish is still popular in Ireland and in most other EC
countries. It is one of those quick and simple recipes, for which you can use grouse or
pheasant if you wish. This is a typical Bagshot Heath recipe, dating back to 1870.
Allow 24 hours for the meat to marinate.

75g/3oz butter, warm
1 clove garlic, crushed
salt and freshly ground black pepper
4 oven-ready wood pigeons, trussed
25g/1oz dripping
175g/6oz wild mushrooms
12 shallots

25g/1oz plain flour
150ml/¼pt brandy
300ml/½pt double cream

Garnish
1 tbsp parsley, freshly chopped

• Place the butter, crushed garlic, salt and freshly ground black pepper in a bowl. Generously rub the mixture inside and out of the pigeons and leave, covered, for 24 hours in a cool place.

• Pre-heat the oven to 230°C/450°F/gas mark 8.

• Heat the dripping in a large roasting tin and quickly seal the pigeons all over, turning them with a carving fork or roasting fork. Bake in the centre of the oven for 40 minutes, basting every 10 minutes. Take the pigeons from the baking tray and allow them to cool slightly on a wire rack.

• Place the juices in a saucepan and cook the mushrooms and shallots for 5 minutes and sprinkle with the flour. Add the warm brandy and ignite, add the cream and cook for 3 minutes on a very low heat, stirring all the time.

• Carefully cut the pigeons into quarters, removing as many bones as you can. Place the pigeons in a casserole dish, cover with the cream sauce and bake in the oven for a further 12 minutes at 170°C/325°F/gas mark 3.

• Sprinkle with freshly chopped parsley and serve with wild rice or roast potatoes and buttered Brussels sprouts.

Rabbit

WITH ROSEMARY AND CIDER SAUCE

A quick and simple recipe, which is great if you have a slow cooker – just throw it in and leave it!

8 slices of streaky bacon, rindless
8 x 175g/6oz rabbit portions
8 wooden cocktail sticks
1 tbsp wild rosemary
1 large onion, peeled and sliced
300ml/½pt dry cider
2 tbsp honey, warm
1 tbsp English mustard

1 tsp tomato purée
salt and freshly ground black pepper
1 tbsp cornflour, mixed with 2 tbsp sherry

Garnish
1 apple, sliced
sprig of fresh rosemary

• Pre-heat the oven to 230°C/450°F/gas mark 8.
• Wrap the bacon around each piece of rabbit and secure with the wooden cocktail sticks. Place the pieces in a deep, buttered casserole and cook for 20 minutes. Remove the cocktail sticks.
• Place the rosemary, onion, cider, honey, mustard, tomato purée, salt and freshly ground black pepper into a bowl and mix thoroughly. Pour the mixture over the rabbit and cover. Lower the oven to 150°C/300°F/gas mark 2 and cook in the centre of the oven for 90 minutes.
• Remove the rabbit and bacon to a warm serving dish, pour the sauce into a saucepan, heat and thicken with the cornflour.
• Pour the hot sauce over the rabbit and garnish with slices of apple and rosemary.

Venison Steak

WITH BLACK CHERRIES

Scotland is a place of true beauty, and some of the finest venison comes from there, although there are a few deer roaming around the backyard of a little house around the corner from my house. Alas, I'm forbidden from going near them while I'm wearing my chef's whites! This recipe takes 48 hours to marinate, but it really is worth the effort.

6 x 225g/8oz slices of venison haunch,
   trimmed and tenderized
6 black peppercorns, crushed
275g/10oz black cherries, pitted
12 shallots, peeled and sliced
4 rashers streaky bacon, rindless and chopped
8 juniper berries
4 tbsp port
150ml/¼pt red wine

salt and freshly ground black pepper
25g/1oz butter
2 tbsp walnut oil
25g/1oz flour

Garnish
black cherries
sprigs of fresh parsley

- Place the slices of venison in a large, deep tray. Add the peppercorns, cherries and juice, shallots, bacon, juniper berries, port and wine. Season well with salt and freshly ground black pepper. Place the venison and marinade in the fridge for 48 hours.
- Pre-heat the oven to 180°C/350°F/gas mark 4.
- Remove the steaks from the marinade and fry them quickly in a large frying pan with the melted butter and walnut oil for 4 minutes either side. Place the steaks back into the marinade (reserving the butter, oil and venison juices in the pan) and bake in the oven, covered with cooking foil, for 40 minutes. Remove the steaks from the tray to a warm serving dish.
- Add the flour to the juices in the frying pan and cook for 4 minutes, add the marinade and bring to the boil. Simmer for 10 minutes until the sauce is smooth. Pour over the venison steaks and serve garnished with black cherries and fresh parsley.

Beetroot and Rhubarb Chutney

This is a taste of the Orient, a cross between sweet and sour with an exciting taste

450g/1lb Red Velvet cooked beetroot, diced
450g/1lb rhubarb (red end), washed and
  chopped
2 onions, chopped
3 tbsp sultanas
1 tbsp green peppercorns in brine

4 tbsp soft brown sugar
pinch of cayenne pepper
1 tsp salt
1 tbsp mild curry paste
2 tbsp port
150ml/¼pt white wine vinegar

- Put all the ingredients in a large saucepan, bring to the boil and simmer slowly for 10 minutes, stirring all the time. Let the mixture stand for 30 minutes.
- Bring back to the boil and simmer for 30 minutes.
- Put into warm jars, allow it to stand for 3 weeks before using.

PIES AND PASTIES

Melton Mowbray Pork Pie

Veal and Ham Pie

Traditional Steak and Kidney Pie

Cheese and Onion Pie

Cumberland Bacon and Egg Pie

Huntingdon Fidget Apple and Pork Pie

Shepherd's Pie

Turkey and Ham Pie

Cornish Pasty

Chicken and Leek Pasty

Apple Pie

Suet Pastry

Shortcrust Pastry

Puff Pastry

I have lifted the lid on some of the most famous pies around the country, and there is not one area of Britain that does not have a pie or pasty associated with it. We automatically think of Melton Mowbray Pie, Cheshire Pork Pie and the Cornish Pasty, and Steak and Kidney is known all over the country, but there are many, many more, and I have included a good selection from my Pie Society Collection in this mouth-watering chapter.

My aim in life is to show that we do have the very best of produce within our shores, and this is one area in which we can show our European neighbours how to make perfect pastry and pies. My ambition is to create at least one pie a month, and I experiment on my children's taste buds as I teach them the art of pie filling.

The author's homemade pies

Melton Mowbray Pork Pie

I am convinced that this became popular not because it was a hunting pie, but because it originated very near to the area in which Stilton was traditionally made. The art of pie making is quite simple: use fresh, high quality ingredients and do as you are told. I have numerous recipes for this pie, but a manuscript copy of an old one beats them all, and I have just been waiting for the right cookery book to put it in. If you don't skimp on this recipe and follow it completely you will not be disappointed.

Stock
pork bones
1 pig's foot
600ml/1pt water
1 large onion, peeled
1 carrot
1 bay leaf
2 sage leaves
sprig of thyme
sprig of marjoram
salt
6 peppercorns

Pie filling
675g/1½lb pork shoulder (one-third fat), skin and gristle removed cut into very small dice, 5mm/¼in
generous pinch of salt
generous pinch of white pepper
1 tsp essence of anchovy

225g/8oz hot-water pastry (see page 85)

1 egg, whisked for glaze

SERVES 6

• Make the stock by putting all the ingredients into a large pan, bring to the boil and simmer for 2 hours or more until the stock has reduced to 300ml/½pt. Let it cool and skim off all the fat. Check the seasoning. When the stock is completely cool, pour it through a fine, non-metallic sieve and place to one side.
• Make the filling by combining all the ingredients in a bowl with 2 tbsp of the stock.
• Make up the hot-water pastry as described for the Veal and Ham Pie (see page 85).
• Place the pie case on a baking tray and put in the pork filling. Top with the pastry lid, firmly crimping the edges but being careful not to break the pie case. Make a hole in the centre of the lid to allow the steam out during the cooking. Bake in the lower part of the oven for 2 hours at 180°C/350°F/gas mark 4. 10 minutes before the end of cooking time, egg glaze the pie and return to the oven.
• Turn off the oven but do not open the door. Leave the pie in the oven to cool naturally for 1 hour. Re-heat the jelly until it is just warm and pour as much stock as the pie will hold through the hole in the lid.
• Let the pie cool completely, wrap it in kitchen film and refrigerate for at least a day. Before serving, take one slice from the pie and hide it from your family so that you can enjoy a reward for all your hard work.

Veal and Ham Pie

Known as the party pie in many pubs and inns, this is ideal for a summer buffet party.

450g/1lb veal, minced
150g/5oz York ham, minced
1 tbsp parsley, chopped
4 tbsp cranberry jelly
rind of 1 lemon, grated
2 onions, skinned, finely chopped
salt and freshly ground black pepper
4 eggs, hard-boiled and shelled
3 tbsp powered aspic jelly
300ml/½pt clear apple juice, warmed

Pastry
150g/5oz lard
200ml/7fl oz hot water
350g/12oz plain flour, seasoned with ½ tsp salt
1 large egg yolk

SERVES 8

- Pre-heat the oven to 180°C/350°F/gas mark 4.
- In a large mixing bowl put the veal, ham, parsley, cranberry jelly, lemon rind and onions, add 1 tsp salt and some freshly ground black pepper. Combine and place to one side.
- Make the pastry by putting the lard and water into a saucepan. Heat gently until the lard has melted. Bring to the boil, remove from the heat and beat in the seasoned flour to form a soft dough. Beat the egg yolk into the dough, cover the dough with a damp cloth and leave to rest in a warm place for 15 minutes, but do not allow the dough to cool. Roll out the pastry and pat two-thirds of the pastry into the base and sides of a 1.2l/2pt loaf tin, greased and lined with greaseproof paper, distributing it evenly to make the shape for the pie filling.
- Place half the meat in the tin. Arrange the eggs down the centre, then top with the remaining meat mixture. Make a lid with the remaining pastry. Cover the pie and seal the edges, using any pastry trimmings to decorate the top.
- Make a large hole in the centre of the pie. Bake for 90 minutes and allow to cool for 3 hours.
- Make up the aspic jelly to 300ml/½pt with apple juice, cool for 10 minutes, then pour the aspic through the hole in the top of the pie. Chill the pie for 2–3 hours, then remove the pie from the tin.
- Slice with a warm carving knife and serve with pickles and a red cabbage salad.

Traditional Steak and Kidney Pie

Everyone's favourite and the most popular pie around Britain, in homes as well as restaurants, cafés and hotels. Do not use cheap cuts of meat. Only the best rump steak and ox kidney will give the perfect pie. If you want to make this into a Steak and Ale Pie, omit the kidney and soak the steak in 150ml/¼pt beer overnight, then use the beer with the stock.

575g/1¼lb rump steak
175g/6oz ox kidney
25g/1oz seasoned flour
25g/1oz butter

1 large onion, chopped
300ml/½pt meat stock
salt and freshly ground black pepper
225g/8oz suet pastry (see page 92)

SERVES 6

• Trim the skin and fat from the steak and cut the meat into 2.5cm/1in cubes. Remove the fat, skin and core from the kidney and cut into quite small cubes. Toss the steak and kidney in the seasoned flour.
• Melt the butter in a large frying pan and quickly seal the meat all over. Add the chopped onion and cook for 4 minutes. Add the stock, season and simmer for a further 25 minutes.
• While the beef is simmering, line a large, well-greased pudding basin with the suet pastry, leaving enough pastry to make a lid. Put the steak, kidney and stock into the basin and top with the lid, damping the edges with water to make it stick.
• Cover the basin with buttered tin foil or greaseproof paper and stand the basin in a large saucepan with enough water to half cover the basin. Bring the water to the boil and steam for 2 hours, making sure that you top up the water so that the pan does not boil dry.
• Serve with fresh carrots and swede mashed with a little butter and nutmeg, garnished with roast potatoes.

Cheese and Onion Pie

There are hundreds of permutations to this pie – simply add leeks for a Likky Pie, grilled streaky bacon for a Bacon and Cheese Pie, cooked minced beef for a Savoury Mince Pie and so on. The basis of every good pie is to season the filling well before putting the lid on.

275g/10oz shortcrust pastry (see page 93)
25g/1oz butter
1 large onion, peeled and chopped
275g/10oz Cheddar cheese, grated
100g/4oz potatoes, cooked and diced

2 eggs, beaten with a little cream
pinch cayenne pepper
salt
1 egg for glaze.

- Pre-heat the oven to 220°C/425°F/gas mark 7.
- Roll out the pastry on to a floured surface, using two-thirds for the base and putting the rest on one side for the topping. Grease and line a pie dish with the pastry.
- Melt the butter in a saucepan and gently fry the onions for about 4 minutes until they are transparent. Allow them to cool, then put them with the cheese and the rest of the ingredients in a large bowl. Mix thoroughly.
- Place the mixture into the lined pie dish and top with the remaining pastry. Glaze with a little egg wash and bake in the oven for 30 minutes until golden-brown.
- For extra flavour add a little sliced apple or leeks.

Cumberland Bacon and Egg Pie

This is one of those recipes of which every county has its own version. Avril Cooper-English, who lives in Staveley near Kendal, Cumbria, is a cook who always produces something memorable. Her husband, Colin, is the creator of some special ice creams, and they have earned him a rosette in Henrietta Green's/BBC Radio 4 *Food Programme* and Food Lovers' Guide to Britain 1996–97. Another version of this pie uses Cumberland sausage, cut into pieces and grilled, instead of the bacon.

225g/8oz shortcrust pastry (see page 93)
175g/6oz streaky bacon, rindless
5 large eggs
4 tbsp double cream

a generous pinch of freshly grated nutmeg
salt and freshly ground black pepper
1 egg to glaze

- Pre-heat the oven to 220°C/425°F/gas mark 7.
- Roll out the pastry, dividing it into 150g/5oz for the base and the rest for the top. Grease and line a deep ovenproof pie dish with the 150g/5oz shortcrust.
- Grill the bacon until crisp, cut it into 2.5cm/1in pieces and scatter over the base of the pie. Break the eggs into the pie leaving them completely whole. Pour over the double cream. Season well with the nutmeg, salt and freshly ground black pepper.
- Moisten the edges of the pie and cover with the remaining pastry. Press the edges together firmly. Decorate the top with little leaf effects with the trimmings from the pastry, glaze with egg and bake in the centre of the oven for 30 minutes until golden-brown.

Huntingdon Fidget Apple and Pork Pie

Served cold with pickles and chunks of cheese, this is a typical farmer's pie. Instead of apples, try using pears with a little Calvados for a flavour with a difference.

900g/2lb pork, rough minced
50g/2oz onion, finely chopped
150ml/¼pt dry white wine
2 tbsp brandy
½ tsp dried sage
1 tbsp Dijon mustard
1 bramley apple, peeled and grated coarsely
salt and freshly ground black pepper

hot-water pastry (see page 85)

Stuffing
175g/6oz packet stuffing (sage and onion)
50g/2oz freshly minced onion
50g/2oz freshly minced bramley apple
blended with 150ml/¼pt beef stock, darkened
  and blended with 225g/8oz black pudding,
  mashed and skin removed

egg to glaze
jelly made with a little wine and pork stock

MAKES 6 INDIVIDUAL PIES

• Pre-heat the oven to 200°C/400°F/gas mark 6.

• Mix the minced pork with the onion, wine, brandy, sage, Dijon mustard and apple, and season this well with a generous pinch of salt and some fresh ground black pepper.

• Line the bottom of each pie mould with hot-water pastry. Quarter fill the lined tins with the meat mixture and then the stuffing mixture, alternating until you have three layers of pork and two of stuffing.

• Roll out the remaining pastry, making the lids to fit the pies. Make a hole in the centre of the lids. Decorate with pastry leaves, egg glaze and bake for 35 minutes. Reduce the oven to 180°C/350°F/gas mark 4 and continue to bake for a further hour.

• Remove the pies from the oven and allow to cool. Pour in some aspic jelly, made up with a little wine and pork stock. When the aspic has set, wrap the pies in kitchen film and leave to mature for 2 days.

Shepherd's Pie

If I had a pint for every argument I have had about this pie, I would own a brewery by now. Shepherd's Pie is made with lamb; Cottage Pie is made with beef. I believe that the meat for a Shepherd's Pie must be cooked, and that is the first stage. I have also added extra flavours, because the original recipes, including Mrs Beeton's of 1861, are rather bland. In the north of England, Shepherd's Pie is always sprinkled with Lancashire cheese before baking and served with red cabbage and sliced beetroot.

25g/1oz dripping
450g/1lb lamb, roughly minced
225g/8oz loin lamb, fat removed and diced
2 large onions, skinned and sliced
2 carrots, peeled and diced
pinch of fresh rosemary
salt
freshly ground black pepper
25g/1oz plain flour

300ml/½pt lamb stock
2 tbsp port
1 tsp Worcestershire sauce
1 tbsp tomato purée
100g/4oz sweet (Chinese) peas
700g/1½lb warm mashed potato, seasoned
  and buttered
25g/1oz butter, softened
75g/3oz crumbly Lancashire cheese

- Pre-heat the oven to 200°C/400°F/gas mark 6.
- Melt the dripping in a large saucepan and fry the lamb for 10 minutes. Add the onions, carrots and rosemary, fry for a further 5 minutes, then season with salt and pepper.
- Add the flour and cook for a further 2 minutes. Very slowly add the stock and port. Finally, add the Worcestershire sauce and tomato purée and cook for a further 25 minutes, stirring every 4 minutes. Blend in the peas and allow the mixture to cool.
- Place the mixture in a deep pie dish and cover with warm mashed potato, using a fork to spread the potato so that it completely covers the meat and vegetable mixture. Sprinkle with softened butter and the crumbled Lancashire cheese and bake in the centre of the oven for 20 minutes.

Turkey and Ham Pie

A real after-Christmas treat, this pie is also popular during the Easter weekend and is often served at picnics and summer fetes. I like to use fresh tarragon in the pie to give it that sweet smell when you cut into it, but you can use another herb if you prefer.

25g/1oz butter
2 carrots, diced
10 button onions, skinned
225g/8oz York ham, shredded
25g/1oz plain wholemeal flour
450ml/15fl oz milk

450g/1lb turkey meat, cut into strips
2 tbsp double cream
salt
freshly ground black pepper
1 tsp tarragon, freshly chopped
275g/10oz puff pastry (see page 93)

SERVES 6

- Pre-heat the oven to 200°C/400°F/gas mark 6.
- Melt the butter in a saucepan, lightly fry the carrots, onions and ham for 5 minutes. Blend in the flour and cook for 1 minute. Slowly add the milk, stirring continuously until the sauce thickens and becomes smooth. Simmer for 3 minutes.
- Add the meat, cream and seasoning. Should you wish to, at this stage sprinkle over your favourite herb.
- Pour the mixture into a 1.2l/2pt pie dish. Roll out the puff pastry to form a lid to fit the pie dish, seal well and brush the top with a little milk.
- Bake for 25–30 minutes until golden-brown, and serve with buttered broccoli and new minted potatoes.

Cornish Pasty

When Florence White (Mary Evelyn) wrote *Good Things in England* in 1932, she suggested that someone should write a book about 'The Pyes of Olde England', and many of my recipes in this section have been inspired by her pioneering writing. The Cornish Pasty is notable because it is one of the few forms of English cookery that conserves all the value of the food. It contains meat, turnip and onion, with the pastry joined at the side, and it was the ultimate portable lunch for the working men of Cornwall. It is very important that the meat and vegetables are cut into small pieces, about 1 x 1 x 1cm/½ x ½ x ½in.

Pastry rolled out like a plate,
Piled with turmut, tates and mate,
Doubled up, and baked like fate,
That's a Cornish pasty.

25g/1oz dripping
350g/12oz rump steak, diced
4 potatoes, peeled and diced
1 large onion, peeled and chopped
1 large carrot, peeled and diced

100g/4oz turnip, diced
1 tbsp parsley
salt and freshly ground black pepper
450g/1lb shortcrust pastry (see page 93)
1 egg beaten with a little milk

MAKES 4–6 PASTIES

- Pre-heat the oven to 220°C/425°F/gas mark 7.
- Heat the dripping in a large saucepan, add the meat and vegetables and cook for 8 minutes, stirring all the time with a wooden spoon. Add the parsley, season the mixture well and allow it to cool completely.
- Roll out the pastry to about 5mm/¼in thick and cut out 4–6 rounds, each 15cm/6in across. Put equal amounts of the mixture into the centre of each round. Dampen the edge of the rounds with beaten egg, fold each round over to make a half-moon shape, and turn the edges round to make small 'horns'. Pinch and crimp the edges to seal the pasty completely. Glaze with beaten egg and place the pasties on a greased baking sheet.
- Bake in the centre of the oven. After 10 minutes lower the temperature to 180°C/350°F/gas mark 4, then cook for 30 minutes.

Forfar Bridies

Invented by Mr Jolly, a Forfar baker, in the 1870s, these are very similar to the Cornish Pasty except they are more of a steak pasty than a Cornish Pasty. They are called Bridies because they are a simple dish, which a young bride could add to her cookery book.

Follow the recipe for the Cornish Pasty, but omit the potato, carrot and turnip. Add a generous pinch of dried English mustard to the seasoning.

Chicken and Leek Pasty

A taste of Wales. An Irish version of this recipe uses diced potatoes with strong onions instead of leeks. When they could not afford chicken, miners used sausage meat.

450g/1lb chicken breast meat, roughly
  chopped
50g/2oz butter
4 leeks, cleaned and finely chopped
2 sprigs fresh parsley

3 tbsp redcurrant jelly
225g/8oz potatoes, cooked and diced
salt and freshly ground black pepper
450g/1lb shortcrust pastry (see page 92)
egg beaten with a little milk

MAKES 6–8 PASTIES

- Pre-heat the oven to 180°C/350°F/gas mark 4.
- Put the chicken meat into a frying pan with the butter, leeks and parsley, cook and cover for 25 minutes, stirring every 5 minutes. Add the redcurrant jelly and potatoes, season well and allow to cool.
- Roll out the pastry to 5mm/¼in thick and cut out 6–8 rounds, each 15cm/6in across. Place the mixture in the centre of each round. Dampen the edges and fold over to make a half-moon shape. Pinch and crimp the edges.
- Glaze with the beaten egg, put the pasties on a greased baking sheet and bake for 35 minutes. Serve with a crisp vegetable salad.

Apple Pie

When you are picking apples, always leave two apples on the tree for good luck – they also help to feed the birds! As a variation, add ripe but firm blackberries. Wash them gently under a spray of cold water, then hull.

450g/1lb shortcrust pastry (see page 93)
450g/1lb apples, peeled, quartered and cored
100g/4oz soft brown sugar
6 cloves, crushed

1 tsp cinnamon
1 egg white, whisked
25g/1oz caster sugar

SERVES 8

• Pre-heat the oven to 200°C/400°F/gas mark 6. Line a large pie dish with two-thirds of the pastry, reserving the remainder for the lid.
• Place the apples, sugar, cloves and cinnamon in the pie dish. Cover the pie with the remaining pastry, sealing the edges and make a small hole in the centre of the pastry.
• Brush with the egg white and sprinkle with caster sugar. Bake for 20 minutes, then reduce the heat to 180°C/350°F/gas mark 4 and bake for a further 20 minutes.
• Remove from the oven, allow to cool for 10 minutes and serve with whipped double cream.

Suet Pastry

No one is a better cook than one's own mother, and my own mother understood perfectly the art of making suet pastry. She once told me: 'Warm hands make a warm heart but not really good pastry.' Suet should be fresh if possible, and it is best to buy it from your butcher. It should be grated on a cheese grater and seasoned with a little salt before use.

225g/8oz self-raising flour
75g/3oz butter, softened
50g/2oz suet, freshly shredded

salt and freshly ground black pepper
1 egg (size 3)
1 tbsp water

MAKES ABOUT 450G/1LB

• Place the flour, butter and suet in a bowl, season with a little salt and freshly ground black pepper. Rub together with your fingertips until the mixture resembles fine breadcrumbs.
• Mix the egg and water together, make a well in the centre of the flour mixture and pour in the egg. Mix together until a soft paste forms. Turn the mixture out on to a floured work surface and knead into a soft but fairly firm dough.

Shortcrust Pastry

Good pastry should be light in texture. It is important that you weigh the ingredients accurately and keep all the ingredients, utensils and your clean hands as cool as possible.

350g/12oz plain flour
½ tsp salt
75g/3oz butter

75g/3oz lard
flour for rolling out

• Sift the flour and salt into a clean bowl, then gently rub in the butter and lard until the mixture resembles fine breadcrumbs.
• Add enough cold water to make a stiff dough. Press the dough together with your fingertips.
• Sprinkle with a little sifted flour, then roll out the pastry on a lightly floured surface. Use as directed in the recipes.

Puff Pastry

When you make puff pastry, it is worth making a large batch and freezing half of it because it is a long drawn out, time-consuming job. It will keep frozen for up to 3 months.

225g/8oz plain flour
½ tsp salt
225g/8oz unsalted butter

150ml/¼pt chilled water
½ tsp lemon juice
flour for rolling

• Sift the flour and salt into a clean bowl. Lightly rub in 50g/2oz of the butter. Add the lemon juice and a little cold water to make a smooth dough.
• Shape the remaining butter into a rectangle, about 12.5 x 10cm/5 x 4in, on a sheet of greaseproof paper.
• Carefully roll out the dough on a lightly floured surface to a strip a little wider than the butter and twice as long.
• Place the butter on half the pastry, gently fold over the other half, pressing the edges with the floured rolling pin. Leave the pastry in a cool place for 20 minutes to allow the butter to harden.
• Roll out the pastry on a lightly floured surface. It is here you must think about thirds. Fold the bottom third up and the top third down, pressing the edges together with the rolling pin. Turn the pastry so that the folded edges are on the right and left of you. Roll and fold again. Cover and leave in a cool place for 15–20 minutes. Repeat this process of rolling out six times.
• Leave the pastry covered in the fridge until it is required.

VEGETABLES

Bridge and Rea's Beetroot and Orange Mould

Creamy Cheese Cabbage or Broccoli Florets

Pan Haggerty

Champ

Bubble and Squeak Vegetable-filled Cakes

Vegetable Casserole

Potato Pancakes

Spinach and Wild Mushroom Bake

Creamed Mushrooms

Welsh Potato and Onion Bake

Only the best British cooks would recognize words like Champ, Pan Haggerty and Squeak. I have put together several famous British vegetable recipes, beginning with an unusual beetroot mould and including Pan Haggerty, which is a succulent dish of layers of potatoes, Cheddar cheese and onions from the northeast of England. There are also some 'healthy eating' ideas and some recipes for vegetarians.

Yvonne with Red Velvet beetroot

Bridge and Rea's Beetroot and Orange Mould

I created this dish with my friend and fellow chef Barry Rea
to complement a lamb dish I am working on at present.

450g/1lb Red Velvet beetroot, cooked and
  finely chopped
300ml/½ pt double cream
4 eggs

pinch of ground rosemary
salt and freshly ground black pepper
1 large orange, cut into segments

• Pre-heat the oven to 140°C/275°F/gas mark 1.
• Make sure that the beetroot is dry and put it and the cream in a food processor.
Blend thoroughly, then pass the mixture through a very fine sieve.
• Whisk the eggs briskly and add them to the beetroot mixture. Add the rosemary
and season well.
• Pour the mixture into a buttered pudding mould. Place the orange segments
around the mould, lengthways down into the beetroot mixture.
• Carefully place the pudding basin in a baking tray half filled with warm water,
cover with cooking foil and bake in the centre of the oven for 60 minutes until the
beetroot mixture is firm to the touch. Allow the mould to cool naturally and serve
warm or cold with your favourite meat or fish recipe.

Creamy Cheese Cabbage or Broccoli Florets

Florence White (Mary Evelyn) was the founder of the English Folk Cookery Association,
and she wrote *Good Things in England* in 1932. I agree with everything she says, except I
would cook cabbage for no more than 8–10 minutes. I remember those school dinners
when it was coated in soda and boiled until it was completely tasteless.

50g/2oz butter
1 large onion, peeled and finely chopped
1 large cabbage, hard core removed, shredded
  and washed or 450g/1lb broccoli florets
150ml/¼ pt vegetable stock, boiling

salt and freshly ground white pepper
1 tbsp plain four
150ml/¼ pt single cream
50g/2oz Cheddar cheese, grated
nutmeg, freshly grated

• Melt half the butter in a large saucepan and cook the onions for 4 minutes. Add
the cabbage or broccoli to the pan and cook for 3 minutes, stirring all the time,
add the hot vegetable stock, bring to the boil and simmer and cook for a further
15 minutes. Season well with salt and freshly ground white pepper.

- Melt the remaining butter in a saucepan, sprinkle with the flour and cook for 2 minutes. Slowly stir in the cream, add the grated cheese, season with salt and a little freshly grated nutmeg.
- Drain the cabbage and onion thoroughly in a colander and add to the cheese sauce. Cook for about 2 minutes. Serve with slices of fresh apple.

Florence White wrote that the best way to cook cabbage was as follows:
1. After washing cabbage, cut it into quarters, remove any old leaves and cut out any tough stems.
2. Throw it into a saucepan of rapidly boiling slightly salted water.
3. On no account must any soda, bicarbonate or kitchen soda of any kind be added: it destroys all the vitamin value of the cabbage.
4. Boil rapidly with the lid off for 10 to 15 minutes; not a minute longer. Ten minutes is the best time. Lift out and drain; and press lightly.
She then goes onto say the water in which cabbage has been boiled in this manner should never be thrown away; it makes a delicate and delicious foundation for soups, sauces and gravies.

Pan Haggerty

This can be either a main dish, eaten with crusty brown bread and butter, or you can use it as a vegetable accompaniment to a main course.

50g/2oz dripping
450g/1lb potatoes, peeled and thinly sliced
450g/1lb onions, peeled and sliced

salt and freshly ground black pepper
175g/6oz Irish Cheddar cheese, grated

- Heat the dripping in a large-based frying pan. Remove the pan from the heat and interlayer the potatoes, onions and cheese, seasoning well with salt and pepper between each layer, ending with a top layer of cheese. Cover and cook the haggerty, gently, for 25 minutes.
- Uncover and brown the top of the dish under a hot grill. Serve the dish straight from the pan.

Champ

This straightforward dish comes from Northern Ireland. Serve it as a meal in itself.

Boil 450g/1lb of Irish potatoes and mash them with 4 tbsp hot milk, 1 onion, chopped and fried in 25g/1oz butter and seasoned well with salt and freshly ground pepper, and 100g/4oz cooked peas blended with a little butter – and you're a Champ.

Bubble and Squeak Vegetable-filled Cakes

I am sure that once you have tried these tasty cakes, you will be making this vegetarian delight for dinner parties and for the family every week. I came up with the idea after talking to vegetarians who were bored with the mundane food that is so often offered to them. Choose your own favourite fillings. The flavour of the bubble and squeak combined with your surprise centre makes this an intriguing recipe.

30ml/1fl oz cooking oil
1 medium onion, skinned and finely chopped
225g/8oz cooked cabbage, finely chopped
450g/1lb potatoes, cooked and mashed
salt and freshly ground black pepper

cooked vegetables for filling
plain flour, sifted
1 egg and a little milk whisked together
sesame seeds or poppy seeds
25g/1oz dripping or lard

• Heat the oil in a large frying pan and add the chopped onion. Cook for 3 minutes, then add the cabbage and cook for a further 3 minutes. Add the potatoes, season with salt and pepper and fry over a medium heat for a further 10 minutes. Blend the mixture while it cooks.
• Remove the mixture from the pan and turn it into a clean glass bowl. Allow the mixture to cool.
• Flour a cutting board and your hands and take about 50g/2oz of the mixture. Roll it into a ball and then flatten it like a pancake. Put your favourite cooked vegetable on the mixture, fold it over, hiding the vegetable in the centre of the mixture.
• Flatten and shape the mixture into little rounds. Flour and egg wash each one, coat with some sesame seeds or poppy seeds, then fry in a little hot dripping for about 3 minutes on each side until golden-brown.

Vegetable Casserole

This well-known British stew is also known as the classic French vegetable stew, ratatouille. I was introduced to this recipe several years ago when I was a very young chef, learning the art of vegetable cookery, and I was taught to cook it for 40–45 minutes. I found it was overcooked, however, and became very sloppy. This makes an ideal vegetarian meal when placed inside an aubergine, topped with grated cheese and then oven baked.

2 large aubergines	1 large onion
3 large courgettes	3 cloves garlic
sea salt	120ml/4fl oz olive oil
6 large tomatoes	50g/2oz tomato purée
1 large green pepper	½ tsp basil
1 large red pepper	salt and freshly ground black pepper

• Cut the ends off the aubergines and courgettes, wash them thoroughly and dry them on kitchen towel. Cut them into 2.5cm/1in slices. To remove the bitter juices from the aubergine, sprinkle the slices with salt and place them in a colander for 20 minutes; rinse before cooking.

• Scald the tomatoes, remove the skins and chop the flesh roughly. Wash the peppers, remove the white inner ribs and all the seeds, cut them into 2.5cm/1in squares. Peel and coarsely chop the garlic and onion.

• Heat the oil in a large saucepan and fry the onion and garlic for 3 minutes. Stir in the remaining vegetables, tomato purée and basil, season well, cover and simmer for 20 minutes, stirring every 5 minutes.

• Serve with, or in, baked jacket potatoes topped with a little sour cream.

Potato Pancakes

Chefs call potato pancakes, which are made from shredded potatoes, by their Swiss name, Rösti. This recipe dates from Edwardian times, and Rosa Lewis used the same method to make potato baskets, into which she placed minted peas or devilled whitebait.

4 large jacket potatoes	salt and freshly ground black pepper
75g/3oz butter	freshly grated nutmeg

• Boil the potatoes in their skins for 10 minutes, then plunge them into cold water and leave them for at least 1 hour to go completely cold. Skin the potatoes and grate them with a coarse grater.

• Melt the butter in a large saucepan. Put the grated potato in small pancake-shaped heaps, sprinkle with salt, pepper and freshly grated nutmeg. Cook for 12 minutes, and as the potatoes brown, turn them over and repeat the process.

• Press down gently on the potato mixture, to release any excess fat and remove to a warm serving plate.

Spinach and Wild Mushroom Bake

This is one of the tastiest vegetarian dishes I know. When you are adding seasoning to vegetables, always check and recheck: remember, you can add a little more seasoning to a recipe but you cannot take it out.

100g/4oz butter
225g/8oz wild mushrooms
2 cloves garlic
100g/4oz shallots
450g/1lb spinach, cooked, drained and finely
   chopped
225g/8oz Irish Cheddar cheese, grated

¼ tsp nutmeg, freshly grated
1 tsp basil
salt and freshly ground black pepper
50g/2oz plain flour
600ml/1pt hot milk
8 sheets lasagne, cooked and drained
50g/2oz Cheshire cheese, grated

- Pre-heat the oven to 200°C/400°F/gas mark 6.
- Trim and clean the mushrooms. Melt 50g/2oz of the butter in a saucepan and gently fry the garlic, shallots and mushrooms for 3 minutes. Blend in the spinach, cheese, nutmeg and basil, season well with salt and freshly ground black pepper and place to one side.
- In another saucepan melt the remaining butter, add the flour and cook for 1 minute. Slowly add the hot milk, whisking until smooth, add 25g/1oz of the Cheshire cheese, season with salt and freshly ground black pepper.
- Spread half the mushroom and spinach mixture in the bottom of a lightly greased ovenproof dish. Add a layer of lasagne, then half the white sauce. Repeat the process. Sprinkle with Cheshire cheese and cook in the oven for 30 minutes until golden-brown. Serve with crusty bread.

Creamed Mushrooms

In Wales, these mushrooms are served with toast.

To ragoo mushrooms

TAKE large mushrooms, peel and take out the inside, broil them in a gridiron, when the outside is brown put them into a tossing pan, with as much water as will cover them, let them stand for ten minutes, then put to them a spoonful of white wine, the same of browning, a very little allegar, thicken it with flour and butter, boil it a little, lay sippets round your dish, and serve it up.

Elizabeth Raffald, 1769

50g/2oz butter
1 tbsp olive oil or walnut oil
6 shallots, peeled and sliced
450g/1lb button mushrooms, sliced
salt and freshly ground black pepper
1 tsp plain flour

150ml/¼pt double cream
2 tbsp port
nutmeg, freshly grated
1 tbsp parsley, freshly chopped
3 slices of white bread, cut into triangles, fried
   in hot dripping

- Heat the butter and oil in a large saucepan, add the shallots and cook for 3 minutes, then add the mushrooms and cook on a low heat for 2 minutes. Season with salt and freshly ground black pepper, sprinkle with a little flour and cook for 1 minute. Add the cream, port and grated nutmeg and cook for 8 minutes on a low heat.
- Sprinkle with chopped parsley and serve with crispy triangles of bread, fried in dripping.

Spinach as a Vegetable

This really is an interesting recipe, especially when you consider what she says at the end – and remember the date she was writing.

1. Wash and pick the spinach carefully (900g/2lb)
2. Throw it into a saucepan with a little salt (1 tsp)
3. Set the pan on the fire (cook slowly) and shake it well.
4. When sufficiently done (4 minutes), beat up the spinach with some butter (50g/2oz) but it must be sent to the table pretty dry. A little cream is an improvement (4 tbsp).

N.B. – It would look well, if pressed into a tin mould in the form of a large leaf, which is now obtainable.

Mrs Mary Eaton, Bungay, Suffolk, 1823

Welsh Potato and Onion Bake

6 large baking potatoes, peeled and finely sliced
2 large onions, peeled and finely sliced
100g/4oz Caerphilly cheese, grated
100g/4oz leeks, finely cut

salt and freshly ground black pepper
150ml/¼pt milk, blended with 1 egg
4 tbsp vegetable stock

- Pre-heat the oven to 200°C/400°F/gas mark 6.
- In a large, shallow, ovenproof dish, alternate the potatoes, onion, cheese and leeks, seasoning each layer. Pour over the milk, egg and vegetable stock.
- Cover and bake in the centre of the oven for 40 minutes, remove the cover and bake for a further 10 minutes.

PUDDINGS AND DESSERTS

Steak and Ale Pudding
Turkey and Chestnut Pudding
Seasoned Yorkshire Pudding with Pork
Traditional Yorkshire Toad
Yorkshire Pudding with Minced Turkey and Onion
Somerset Breakfast Pudding
Cumberland Rum Nicky
Old-fashioned English Trifle
Fruity Fritters
Cabinet Pudding
Manchester Pudding
Cumberland Pudding
Ginger Pudding with Damson Compote
Bread and Butter Pudding
Newmarket Pudding
Newcastle Chocolate Pudding
Bakewell Pudding
Oxford Orange Tart
Snowdon Pudding
Blueberry Tart
Icky's Sticky Toffee Pudding
David Alton's Cheshire Steamed Ginger Pudding
Treacle Pudding

Puddings, sweet and savoury, have always been an important element in traditional cooking in these islands. The essence of pudding is the use of suet – originally beef suet, but you can easily substitute vegetable suet – to produce a fluffy consistency that will readily absorb flavours. Steamed or boiled, puddings fed rich and poor alike for centuries. In fact, the word 'pudding' came to cover all kinds of dishes that were not, strictly, puddings at all.

I am beginning this selection with a few traditional savouries, including Steak and Ale Pudding and Somerset Breakfast Pudding. I have also included some Victorian favourites as well as some wonderful puddings from all around Britain.

Rum Nicky and Shortbread

Steak and Ale Pudding

Every café in Britain used to make its own version of steak pudding, which would be served with lashings of thick gravy. Try my version, which is on the menu every night at Gallagher's Restaurant in Little Scotland near Blackrod, Lancashire. There is no finer taste than the combination of Guinness, steak and kidney with a suet pastry case. Developing this recipe for Ann and Pat Gallagher, whose menu is a combination of only the best of British food, was time consuming but worth all the hours taken to make this, their signature dish.

450g/1lb suet pastry (see page 92)
flour
1 tsp butter
450g/1lb rump of beef, trimmed weight, cut into cubes
225g/8oz ox kidney, trimmed weight, diced
1 large onion, peeled and finely chopped

1 tbsp plain flour
salt and freshly ground black pepper
1 tbsp Worcestershire sauce
1 tbsp mushroom ketchup
5 tbsp Guinness or stout
300ml/½pt good meat stock
milk

• On a floured board roll out the pastry. Reserve one-third to top the pudding. Use the butter to grease 1.7l/3pt pudding basin and line it with suet pastry, pressing it against the sides and covering the basin completely, with dough over-lapping the edge of the basin.
• Place the beef, kidney and onion in a bowl and sprinkle with flour, seasoning with the salt and freshly ground black pepper. Place the rest of the ingredients in the bowl and blend thoroughly.
• Put the meat filling mixture into the pastry-lined pudding basin. Moisten the edge of the pastry with a little milk and place the pastry top on the pudding, pressing and sealing the edges together. Trim off any excess pastry. Cover the basin with generously greased greaseproof paper and tie it tightly with string.
• Place the pudding in a large pan with enough boiling water to cover two-thirds of the basin. Bring to the boil for 15 minutes, then reduce the heat and steam gently for 4 hours. Remove the greaseproof paper.
• Place a large serving plate on the top of the pudding, then, holding the pudding and plate, turn the pudding onto the plate and serve.

Turkey and Chestnut Pudding

It was easier to steam puddings than to bake pies in Edwardian times, when a pot could be placed over the fire. This pudding used to be called Swan Pudding, then it became Goose and Chestnut to Taste like Swan Pudding. The thought of cooking a beautiful bird like a swan appals me, but when I tried the recipe with goose I found it was not the right meat, so I replaced it with turkey, which was used on a regular basis in Norfolk. This recipe was a particular favourite of the Prince Regent.

500g/1lb suet pastry (see page 92)
500g/1lb turkey meat, diced
225g/8oz streaky bacon, rindless, diced
1 onion, peeled, finely chopped
1 tbsp plain flour
2 tbsp chopped parsley
pinch of nutmeg

225g/8oz chestnuts, weighed with shells
  removed
salt
freshly ground black pepper
3 tbsp brandy
1 tsp clear honey, warmed
300ml/½pt chicken stock

SERVES 6

Follow the recipe for Steak and Ale Pudding (page 104). Instead of turkey and chestnuts, use chicken and ham.

Seasoned Yorkshire Pudding with Pork

It is far better if you use sweet, dessert apples and not a cooking apple, like a bramley, for this recipe.

25g/1oz dripping
350g/12oz pork fillet, cubed and seasoned
1 large onion, finely chopped

1 tbsp freshly chopped sage
Yorkshire pudding batter (see page 24)
4 tbsp apple, freshly chopped

- Pre-heat the oven to 220°C/425°F/gas mark 7.
- Heat the dripping in a large frying pan, add the seasoned pork, onion and sage and cook for 4 minutes.
- Put the fat in a baking tray and place it in the oven for 3 minutes until the fat is smoking. Pour over the batter and sprinkle the pork, sage and onion with finely chopped apple.
- Bake for 30 minutes and serve with apple sauce and a glass of cider.

Traditional Yorkshire Toad

The word 'toad' is popular all over England for a quick and simple lunch or supper. If you don't like beef, try your favourite cut of meat, poultry or game, but make sure that the meat is at least half-cooked before you add it to the baking tin.

25g/1oz dripping
350g/12oz chuck steak, fat and gristle
  removed and cubed

salt and freshly ground black pepper
Yorkshire pudding batter (see page 24)

- Pre-heat the oven to 230°C/450°F/gas mark 8.
- Heat the dripping in a baking tin until it is just smoking. Pour in a quarter of the batter and bake for 10 minutes until the batter is just set. While the batter is baking, season and lightly fry the meat. Add the meat to the baking tin, pour in the remainder of the batter and return to the oven and bake for 20 minutes.
- Reduce the heat (without opening the oven) to 200°C/400°F/gas mark 6 for 15 minutes. Serve with a red wine sauce or onion gravy.

Yorkshire Pudding
WITH MINCED TURKEY AND ONION

I believe that this recipe started its life with mutton, then rabbit, then beef, so you can please yourself. I've used turkey breast.

25g/1oz dripping
225g/8oz minced turkey breast
1 onion, finely chopped

seasoning
Yorkshire pudding batter (see page 24)

- Pre-heat the oven to 220°C/425°F/gas mark 7.
- Heat the dripping in a large frying pan, add the minced turkey and chopped onion and cook for 12 minutes.
- Place a large baking tray and the fat from the minced beef into the oven for 3 minutes until it is very hot – the fat should be smoking. Pour over the batter and sprinkle with the minced turkey and onion.
- Bake for 30 minutes and serve with a rich gravy.

Somerset Breakfast Pudding

There was a shortage of bacon during the war, although American and Canadian bacon could be found for the right price. I have converted this humble wartime recipe so that you can enjoy it.

100g/4oz shredded vegetable suet
350g/12oz plain flour
1 tsp baking powder
75g/3oz potato, grated
salt
1 egg
275g/10oz middle-cut bacon, rindless, grilled
  until crisp and chopped

175g/6oz button mushrooms, sliced
3 tbsp honey, warmed
2 eggs beaten with a little milk
salt
freshly ground black pepper

- Place the suet, flour and baking powder in a large bowl and mix the ingredients together. Add the raw potato, salt and egg with a little water to make the suet pastry. Roll out the suet pastry on a floured board. Grease a medium size pudding basin with a little butter and line the basin with a quarter of the pastry.
- Place the chopped bacon, mushrooms, honey and egg into another bowl and blend the mixture together, seasoning well with salt and pepper.
- Place one-third of the mixture in the bottom of the pudding basin and top with another layer of suet. Repeat this process two more times, finishing with the final layer of suet. Cover that with a layer of well-greased, greaseproof paper, tie it tight with string and steam for 3 hours.

Cumberland Rum Nicky

Colin Cooper-English is well known for his famous homemade ice cream, and he worked with me on *Dr William Kitchiner: Regency Eccentric*, the first biography of the celebrated doctor. Whenever I visit Colin and his wife Avril, who makes the most wonderful shortbread, I have a craving to try his Rum Nicky with liquorice ice cream. The recipe for Rum Nicky is hardly ever seen these days, and the art of making it perfect, says Colin, is to be generous with the rum and to soak the dates and currants in the rum overnight. I have seen four very different recipes for Rum Nicky, using dates, apple, sultanas and currants, but this recipe has just enough currants and dates.

175g/6oz currants
175g/6oz dates, stoned and roughly chopped
150ml/¼pt dark rum
350g/12oz shortcrust pastry (see page 93)

75g/3oz butter
75g/3oz soft brown sugar
1 tsp nutmeg, freshly grated
1 tsp ginger, freshly grated

• Pre-heat the oven to 190°C/375°F/gas mark 5. Soak the currants and chopped dates in the rum overnight.
• Roll out the pastry and use two-thirds to line a large greased pie dish. Roll out the top for the pie and place to one side.
• Cream the sugar and butter together with the nutmeg and ginger. Place the currants and dates in the pastry case and dot with pieces of the creamed butter. Wet the pastry edges with the left-over rum and top with the shortcrust pastry.
• Bake in the centre of the oven for 40 minutes. Allow to cool for 5 minutes, pour the remaining rum over the pastry and serve with clotted cream.

Old-fashioned English Trifle

8 individual sponge fingers
4 tbsp raspberry jam
3 tbsp cream sherry
2 tbsp brandy
25g/1oz flaked almonds

rind of ½ lemon, grated
Custard Sauce (see below)
300ml/½pt double cream
25g/1oz crushed almonds
glacé cherries

• Take the sponge fingers and coat them with the jam. Arrange them in a glass dish and sprinkle with sherry, brandy, almonds and the lemon rind.
• Make the custard and strain it over the sponge fingers. Leave the custard to go quite cold.
• Whip the cream until it is stiff and spread it over the cold custard. Decorate with the crushed almonds and glacé cherries.

CUSTARD SAUCE

2 fresh eggs yolks
25g/1oz caster sugar
3 drops of vanilla essence

300ml/½pt fresh milk, hot
double cream (optional)

• Mix the yolks, sugar and essence in a large, clean bowl. Whisk in the boiled milk. Return the custard to the saucepan and re-heat, stirring all the time with a wooden spoon on a very low heat. Do not allow to boil, or the eggs will become scrambled. At the very end add a little double cream, for extra creaminess.
• For a Christmas Brandy Sauce omit the vanilla essence and add 3 tbsp of brandy. For Whisky or Rum Custard simply add 2 tbsp of the appropriate spirits at the end of cooking and whisk gently before serving.

Fruity Fritters

Until recently, this recipe was a closely guarded secret, known only to
Ma Walsh of Shipley, Yorkshire, who was renowned for her fritter batter.

25g/1oz yeast
150ml/¼ pt warm milk
225g/8oz plain flour
50g/2oz currants
50g/2oz caster sugar
2 medium sized apples, cored, peeled and grated

25g/1oz candied peel
a pinch of nutmeg, freshly grated
2 large eggs, whisked with 1 tbsp sherry
50g/2oz dripping
25g/1oz butter

• Into a large bowl put the yeast and warm milk, whisk until the yeast dissolves,
then leave it to stand for a few minutes.
• Sift the flour with all the other dry ingredients into another bowl. Add the eggs
and blend. Slowly add enough milk to make a thick paste, then add the rest of the
milk to make a creamy batter. Let the batter stand for at least 24 hours.
• Slowly whisk the batter. Heat the dripping and butter in a large pan until it is
hot, then add 1 tbsp of the batter mix at a time to the hot fat. Fry for 2 minutes
each side until golden-brown, drain onto some clean kitchen towel, sprinkle with
sugar and serve warm.

Cabinet Pudding

25g/1oz butter
100g/4oz raisins
4 slices white bread, crust removed and cut
  into 5mm/¼ in cubes

400ml/14fl oz milk
3 large eggs
25g/1oz caster sugar
1 tsp lemon rind, freshly grated

• Lightly butter a 1l/1¾ pt pudding basin and decorate the base and sides by
pressing on firmly 25g/1oz raisins. Put the pieces of bread into a bowl, gently
heat the milk; do not let it boil.
• Place the eggs and sugar in another bowl and mix them together. Add the milk,
the remaining raisins and lemon rind. Pour the mixture over the bread and leave it
to stand for 15 minutes. Pour the bread mixture into the pudding basin, cover
with greaseproof paper or buttered cooking foil and secure with string.
• Place it into a steamer or into a saucepan half-filled with water, cover with a lid
and steam gently for 80 minutes, topping up with water when necessary.
• Remove the pudding and allow it to stand for 5 minutes, then turn out and
serve with warm strawberry jam or Custard Sauce (see page 108).

Manchester Pudding

Every body knows that Manchester is famous for its football teams, Granada Television and *Coronation Street*, but did you also know it has a very famous pudding?

225g/8oz puff pastry (see page 93 or buy frozen)
250ml/8fl oz milk
4 strips of lemon rind
75g/3oz white breadcrumbs

2 large eggs
2 egg yolks
50g/2oz butter, softened
25g/1oz caster sugar
4 tbsp strawberry jam

- Pre-heat the oven to 200°C/400°F/gas mark 6.
- Roll out the pastry on a floured surface and line a 750ml/1½pt pie dish with the pastry.
- Put the milk and lemon rind in a saucepan and heat gently, but do not boil. Remove the pan from the heat and leave the milk and lemon to infuse for 15 minutes.
- Place the breadcrumbs in a bowl and strain the lemon-flavoured milk over them. Return the mixture to the saucepan and simmer for 3 minutes.
- Blend the eggs and egg yolks into the mixture, with the softened butter and sugar.
- Spread the strawberry jam over the base of the pastry. Pour in the breadcrumb mixture and bake for 10 minutes. Lower the heat on the oven to 180°C/350°F/gas mark 4 and bake for 1 hour. Leave the pudding to cool and serve with custard.

Cumberland Pudding

450g/1lb cooking apples, peeled, cored and roughly chopped
100g/4oz shredded vegetable suet
200g/7oz plain flour
2 tsp baking powder
150g/5oz currants

75g/3oz soft brown sugar
nutmeg, freshly grated
2 eggs, beaten
5 tbsp milk
25g/1oz butter
soft, light brown sugar

- Place the apples, suet, flour, baking powder, currants, sugar and freshly grated nutmeg into a large bowl and mix well. Add the beaten eggs with the milk and blend thoroughly. Leave the mixture to stand for 1 hour.
- Grease a 750ml/1½pt pudding basin with the butter. Give the pudding mixture a final stir and pour it into the greased pudding basin. Cover the pudding basin with a piece of buttered greaseproof paper or cooking foil and secure it with string.
- Place the basin in a large saucepan and fill it with boiling water to just one-third from the top of the basin. Cover the pan tightly and steam gently for 2 hours, topping up with water whenever necessary.
- Leave the pudding to stand for 10 minutes then turn it out onto a warm serving plate and sprinkle with the soft brown sugar.

Ginger Pudding
WITH DAMSON COMPOTE

200g/7oz plain flour
1 tsp ground ginger
pinch of salt
1 tsp bicarbonate of soda
100g/4oz vegetable suet, shredded

75g/3oz caster sugar
1 tbsp black treacle
1 tsp ginger, freshly grated
1 egg, beaten with 3 tbsp milk
25g/1oz butter

• Sift the flour, ground ginger, salt and soda into a mixing bowl, add the suet and sugar and mix lightly with your fingers.

• Pour the treacle into a separate bowl, add the freshly grated ginger and the eggs and milk and whisk it all together, then pour the liquid onto the dry ingredients. Blend all the ingredients together to give a soft mixture.

• Grease a 1l/1¾ pt pudding basin with some butter and pour in the mixture. Cover the basin with greaseproof paper or cooking foil and secure with string.

• Place the pudding in a large saucepan and steam the pudding for 2 hours, topping up with water if necessary. Leave to stand for 10 minutes, then place on a warm serving plate. Remove the ginger sauce and serve with a compote of damsons and double cream, garnished with fresh strawberries, raspberries and frosted leaves.

Bread and Butter Pudding

Another way of adding extra flavour to this recipe is to butter the bread,
then spread on your favourite jam.

50g/2oz butter
12 slices of bread, buttered
175g/6oz sultanas
1 nutmeg, freshly grated

400ml/14fl oz milk
2 large eggs
25g/1oz brown sugar
25g/1oz granulated sugar

• Pre-heat the oven to 180°C/350°F/gas mark 4.
• Butter a 2l/3½pt pie dish, cut the bread into triangles and arrange in layers,
butter side up, sprinkled with sultanas and then grated nutmeg; repeat the process.
• Heat the milk in a saucepan, but do not let it boil. Place the eggs in a bowl with
the brown sugar, beat with a whisk and slowly add the hot milk. Pour the egg
mixture over the bread, sprinkle with granulated sugar and grated nutmeg and
leave to stand for 45 minutes.
• Bake in the centre of the oven for 40 minutes until the custard in the bread and
butter pudding is set.

Newmarket Pudding

25g/1oz butter
5 tbsp redcurrant jelly
6 individual trifle sponges
50g/2oz cut mixed peel
50g/2oz raisins

25g/1oz currants
3 eggs, beaten with a few drops of vanilla
    essence
400ml/7fl oz hot milk

• Grease a 13cm/5in round cake tin with the butter, warm the redcurrant jelly
and pour it into the bottom of the cake tin. Cut the trifle sponge vertically into
1cm/½in slices, then alternate layers of trifle sponge and fruits in the cake tin.
• Whisk together the eggs and hot milk (not boiling) and pour over the sponge
and fruit. Allow to stand for 30 minutes. Cover the top of the cake tin with
greaseproof paper or buttered cooking foil and secure with string. Steam or place
the cake tin into a saucepan, add enough boiling water to come halfway up the
sides of the cake tin, cover the pan tightly with a lid and steam over a gentle heat
for 1 hour.
• Remove the pudding and let it stand for 5 minutes, then turn it onto a warm
plate and serve with clotted cream.

Newcastle Chocolate Pudding

25g/1oz butter
50g/2oz plain chocolate, grated
125ml/4fl oz fresh milk
40g/1½oz butter

40g/1½oz caster sugar
2 eggs, separated
100g/4oz white breadcrumbs
½ tsp baking powder

- Butter the inside of a 1l/1¾pt pudding basin.
- Place the grated chocolate and milk into a saucepan and heat slowly to dissolve and blend the chocolate with the milk.
- Place the butter and sugar into a bowl and cream them together. Beat in the egg yolks. Add the melted chocolate mixture, blend in the breadcrumbs and the baking powder.
- In a separate bowl whisk the egg whites until they are stiff and carefully fold them into the pudding mixture. Spoon the mixture in the greased pudding basin and cover with greaseproof paper or cooking foil, secure it with string and place the basin into a pan half-filled with boiling water, place on a tight-fitting lid and gently simmer for 80 minutes.
- Let the pudding stand for 10 minutes, then carefully turn onto a warm serving plate and serve with rich chocolate sauce.

Bakewell Pudding

This version of the famous recipe is delicious served with warm honey.

225g/8oz shortcrust pastry (see page 93)
3 tbsp raspberry jam
50g/2oz butter
50g/2oz caster sugar

1 large egg
50g/2oz cake crumbs
50g/2oz ground almonds
vanilla essence

- Pre-heat the oven to 200°C/400°F/gas mark 6.
- Make the pastry and roll it out on a lightly floured surface. Place an 18cm/7in flan ring on a non-stick baking sheet. Line the flan ring with the pastry. Spread the jam on the base of the pastry.
- Blend the butter and sugar together in a bowl, beat in the egg, cake crumbs, almonds and a few drops of vanilla essence, mixing well. Pour the mixture into the lined pastry and bake in the centre of the oven for 30 minutes.

Oxford Orange Tart

This recipe was a great favourite of George III and Queen Charlotte.

225g/8oz shortcrust pastry (see page 93)
rind of 3 large oranges, finely grated
rind, finely grated, and juice of 1 lemon
400ml/14fl oz fresh orange juice

150g/5oz caster sugar
3 tbsp cornflour
5 large eggs, separated

• Pre-heat the oven to 200°C/400°F/gas mark 6. Line a flan tin with the pastry and bake blind.
• Mix together the orange and lemon rinds, orange juice, 100g/4oz of sugar and the cornflour in a saucepan. Blend thoroughly with a whisk and slowly bring to the boil, stirring constantly. Remove from the heat and stir in the lemon juice and 5 egg yolks. Pour the orange sauce mixture into the baked pastry case.
• Lower the oven temperature to 150°C/300°F/gas mark 2.
• In a separate bowl beat the egg whites and remaining sugar until they are peaky. Place the meringue on top of the pie filling, covering it completely, using a fork to form little peaks. Return the tart to the oven and bake for 25–30 minutes.

Snowdon Pudding

25g/1oz butter
50g/2oz glacé cherries, halved
100g/4oz raisins
100g/4oz white breadcrumbs
100g/4oz vegetable suet, shredded
25g/1oz ground rice

100g/4oz caster sugar
grated rind of 1 lemon
pinch of salt
2 tbsp marmalade
2 eggs beaten with 5 tbsp milk

• Grease a 1l/1¾ pt pudding basin with the butter and decorate the base with half of the glacé cherries and some raisins.
• Put the rest of the cherries, raisins, breadcrumbs, suet, rice, sugar, lemon rind, salt and marmalade in a bowl, blending all the ingredients together. Add the beaten egg and milk and mix the ingredients to form a soft paste mixture, then spoon it into the pudding basin, cover with greaseproof paper or cooking foil and secure it with string.
• Place the basin into a half-filled pan of boiling water, cover with a tight-fitting lid and steam for 2–2½ hours.
• Let it stand for 10 minutes, then turn out onto a warm plate and serve with whisky sauce.

Blueberry Tart

225g/8oz shortcrust pastry (see page 93)
900g/2lb fresh blueberries
75g/3oz caster sugar
1 tbsp plain flour
1 tsp lemon rind

1 tbsp lemon juice
1 tbsp butter
5 fl oz double cream
6 small fresh mint leaves

• Pre-heat the oven to 200°C/400°F/gas mark 6.
• Roll out the pastry on a lightly floured surface and use to line a buttered 20cm/8in flan tin. Bake blind in the centre of the oven for 12 minutes.
• Place three quarters of the blueberries, sugar, flour, lemon rind and juice in a bowl and mix thoroughly. Spoon the mixture into the baked pastry case and dot with the remaining butter. Lower the oven temperature to 150°C/300°F/gas mark 2. Return the tart to the oven and bake for 25 minutes.
• Remove the tart from the oven and allow to stand for 10 minutes.
• Carefully remove 2 tbsp juice. Place the remaining blueberries on top, reserving 6. Serve with cream swirled with blueberry juice and garnish with berries and mint.

Icky's Sticky Toffee Pudding

Of all my years in the industry, working with chefs young and old, the name Francis Coulson more than any other is associated with traditional British food at its best, and no better person than Francis himself could make this classic dish, for which Sharrow Bay Country House Hotel in the Lake District is so greatly renowned.

Sponge
50g/2oz best butter
180g /6oz granulated sugar
2 fresh eggs
180g /6oz dates, chopped
300ml/½ pt water
1 tsp bicarbonate of soda

180g /6oz self-raising flour
vanilla essence

Sauce
600ml/1pt double cream
75g/3oz demerara sugar
1 tbsp black treacle

• Pre-heat the oven to 180°C/350°F/gas mark 4.
• Make the sponge by creaming the butter and sugar together in a large clean bowl. Boil the dates in 300ml/½ pt of water with the bicarbonate of soda. Beat the eggs into the butter, gradually adding the flour, dates and water from the dates with a few drops of vanilla essence. Pour the mixture into a greased baking tin and bake for 40–45 minutes.
• Make the sauce. Put all the ingredients in a large saucepan and bring to the boil, then simmer for 10 minutes until reduced.
• Pour over the sponge and place it under a grill, until it bubbles. Serve with a little double cream or fromage frais.

David Alton's Cheshire Steamed Ginger Pudding

225g/8oz strong white flour
1 tsp ground ginger
1 tsp baking powder
pinch of salt
75g/3oz fresh white breadcrumbs
100g/4oz vegetable suet

100g/4oz caster sugar
1 egg, lightly beaten
100ml/2fl oz fresh milk

3 tbsp homemade blackcurrant and port jam

- Sift the flour, ground ginger, baking powder and a generous pinch of salt into a clean mixing bowl. Add the breadcrumbs, suet and sugar. Mix well. Stir the egg into the mixture and sufficient milk to make a soft dough. Let the pudding mixture rest for 10 minutes, then blend thoroughly.
- Butter a large pudding basin and place a generous tablespoon of jam into the bottom. Spoon in the sponge mixture until the basin is nearly full. Cover with strong greaseproof paper or foil and secure with string.
- Place the pudding in a steamer over a saucepan half-filled with water, cover the pan with a tightly fitting lid and steam for 2 hours, topping up the pan every 30 minutes.
- Heat the rest of the jam and pour over the base of a serving dish. Loosen the sides of the pudding dish carefully with a knife and turn out the pudding onto the jam.

Treacle Pudding

This always reminds me of school dinners, green gym knickers
and over-cooked cabbage.

25g/1oz butter
75g/3oz breadcrumbs
grated rind of 1 lemon
200g/7oz treacle or golden syrup

Suet crust pastry
300g/11oz plain flour
pinch of salt
2 tsp baking powder
150g/3oz shredded suet
flour

- Lightly grease a 1l/1¾pt pudding basin and prepare a large saucepan, half-filled with boiling water and a tight-fitting lid.
- To make the pastry sift the flour, salt and baking power into a clean, dry mixing bowl. Add the suet and about 250ml/8fl oz cold water to make a dough, then divide the dough into two onto a floured surface. Roll out the first portion to make a round 1cm/½ in larger than the top of the pudding basin. Place the pastry into the basin and press it to mould all around the inside of the basin, easing it evenly up the sides to the top.
- Use the remaining portion of pastry to make a lid to fit the top of the basin and the rest to make two rounds to fit the basin at two levels.
- Place a layer of treacle onto the base of the pudding, sprinkle with some of the breadcrumbs and lemon rind, cover with a pastry round and repeat the process until all the ingredients are used, finishing with the pastry lid.
- Cover the pudding with greaseproof paper or cooking foil and secure with string. Place the pudding in the saucepan with the boiling water, secure the lid and steam for 2½ hours.
- Leave to stand for 10 minutes and then carefully turn the pudding out onto a warm serving plate and serve with double cream or vanilla ice cream.

CAKES AND BISCUITS

Date and Almond Cake

Malvern Cherry and Lemon Cake

Elizabeth Raffald's Eccles Cakes

Shortbread Layered with Fresh Strawberries

The Nanny Brow Hazelnut Tart

Newburgh Cinnamon and Chocolate Chip Biscuits

Maids of Honour

Pear Sponge

Manx Cake

Singing Hinnys

I have found recipes dating back from the fifteenth century for this section. Homemade cakes and biscuits always remind me of my grandmother cooking in her little back kitchen in Bolton. Whenever I visited her with my mother when I was a child, the smell of home baking seemed to fill the house.

A selection of British cakes

Date and Almond Cake

Nicholas Lander, who wrote the foreword to this book, says that British produce is now more readily appreciated outside Britain than within. Our American cousins should really appreciate this recipe.

150g/6oz almonds, blanched and sliced
3 eggs
140g/5oz caster sugar
50g/2oz plain flour
½ tsp baking powder
pinch of salt

75g/3oz butter
5 tbsp Amaretto
100g/4oz dates, stoned and chopped
296ml/10fl oz double cream

• Pre-heat the oven to 180°C/350°F/gas mark 4.
• Lightly grease a 20cm/8in cake tin with butter and line the bottom with grease-proof paper. Sprinkle some of the almonds (about 50g/2oz) onto the base of the cake tin. Melt 75g/3oz butter in a pan over a low heat.
• Whisk the eggs and sugar together, sift in the flour, baking powder and salt. Then add the melted butter and blend in 2 tbsp Amaretto, dates and almonds.
• Pour the mixture into the cake tin and bake in the centre of the oven for 35 minutes. Allow the cake to cool for 10 minutes in the cake tin, then loosen the sides with a knife. Turn out onto a cooling rack – the almonds sprinkled onto the base should now be at the top of the cake.
• Whisk 296ml/10fl oz double cream with 3 tbsp Amaretto to make a wonderfully flavoured cream to serve with this cake.

Malvern Cherry and Lemon Cake

Worcester is famous for Royal Worcester china and Malvern is famous for its mineral water and this very light cake.

225g/8oz soft butter
225g/8oz caster sugar
4 eggs, beaten
1 lemon rind, thinly sliced, and juice
275g/10oz glacé cherries

350g/12oz self-raising flour
3 tbsp fresh milk
icing sugar
candied lemon

- Pre-heat the oven to 190°C/375°F/gas mark 5. Grease and line a round cake tin.
- Cream the butter and sugar together until fluffy, then slowly add the eggs and lemon juice and thin slices of rind. Toss the cherries in flour and place on one side. Sift the flour into the mixture. Add the cherries and slowly add the milk.
- Pour the mixture into the cake tin and bake for 30 minutes until it is well risen and firm to the touch. Turn the cake onto a wire rack and allow it to cool. Lightly dust with icing sugar and decorate with candied lemon.

Elizabeth Raffald's Eccles Cakes

Everywhere I go I am asked about the origins of Eccles Cakes, and I am constantly being asked by bakeries to recreate this recipe for them. Whenever people come to my home, they think they can smell them being made. Eccles Cakes and Hawkshead, Banbury, Chorley, Newburgh and Coventry Godcakes all belong to the same class. They consist of short or puff pastry. The Eccles Cake, like the Newburgh Cake, is smaller than the Chorley Cake, but each kind is filled with a special mixture. Here is the recipe of the mother of English cookery, Elizabeth Raffald (1733–81), who invented the Eccles Cake.

25g/1oz best butter
100g/4oz currants
25g/1oz mixed peel
50g/2oz mixed fruit
50g/2oz demerara sugar
½ tsp mixed spice

½ tsp ginger, freshly grated
½ tsp nutmeg, freshly grated
225g/8oz puff pastry (see page 93)
1 egg white, lightly whisked
50g/2oz caster sugar

- Pre-heat the oven to 220°C/425°F/gas mark 7.
- Melt the butter in a saucepan and add all the ingredients, except the pastry, egg white and caster sugar. Blend and cook for 4 minutes. Allow to cool.
- Roll out the puff pastry until it is very thin. Use a large pastry cutter to cut it into rounds. Place a good tbsp of the mixture onto each round. Gather up the edges, turn over and press with a rolling pin into a flat cake, then shape back into a round.
- Place them on a dampened baking sheet. Brush the tops lightly with the egg white and sprinkle with caster sugar. Lower the oven temperature to 200°C/400°F/gas mark 6 and bake for 18–20 minutes in the centre of the oven until golden-brown.

> For an even lighter pastry leave it in the refrigerator overnight. Eccles cakes are ideal with a little butter, English cheeses garnished with grapes, spring onions, radishes, baby beetroot and celery or for a special afternoon treat.

Shortbread Layered with Fresh Strawberries

225g/8oz plain flour
100g/4oz best butter, softened
50g/2oz caster sugar
1 egg, separated

caster sugar for sieving
icing sugar
450g/1lb fresh strawberries, hulled and
   halved, soaked in your favourite liqueur

• Pre-heat the oven to 200°C/400°F/gas mark 6.
• Into a large bowl put the flour and softened butter, rubbing gently with your fingertips until the mixture resembles breadcrumbs. Add the sugar, blending thoroughly, then add the egg yolk to bind the mixture together.
• Knead the mixture lightly on a floured board, then roll it out to about 5mm/¼in thick. Prick the surface with a fork, then use a 7.5.cm/3in fluted cutter to cut out 12 rounds. Place the rounds on a greased baking tray, brush lightly with the egg white and sprinkle with caster sugar.
• Bake for 25 minutes, until they are a light golden-brown. Transfer to a wire rack to cool.
• Place one biscuit in the centre of a plate and cover evenly with strawberries, top with another biscuit and repeat the process. Dust the third biscuit with icing sugar. Garnish with a fan of strawberries and other berries.

The Nanny Brow Hazelnut Tart

There are always some recipes that everyone would like to have in their cookery collection and this is one of my personal favourites. Head Chef Shona and her Pastry Chef Joe spend many happy hours at the Nanny Brow Country House in the Lakes creating tempting desserts for their clientele.

2 tbsp plain flour
225g/8oz shortcrust pastry (see page 93. Add
1 tsp of ground ginger to the dry pastry mix)
450g/1lb whole hazelnuts
4 eggs

225g/8oz soft brown sugar
170g/6oz golden syrup or clear honey
50g/2oz butter, melted
vanilla essence

- Pre-heat the oven to 200°C/400°F/gas mark 6. On a floured surface (2 tbsp flour), roll out and line a flan tin (20cm/8in) with the pastry and bake blind for 10 minutes.
- Chop half the nuts. In a large bowl, whisk the eggs, add the sugar, syrup or honey, melted butter, vanilla essence and sift in the remaining flour, blending thoroughly.
- Scatter the chopped nuts over the cooked pastry case and pour over the mixture. Then scatter the remaining whole hazelnuts over the top.
- Bake in the centre of the oven for 10 minutes; then lower the oven temperature to 170°C/325°F/gas mark 3 for 35 minutes.

Newburgh Cinnamon and Chocolate Chip Biscuits

I created this biscuit for Newburgh Fair in Lancashire when I was
organizing my annual barbecue for the local school.
They sold out, and if you try them yourself, you will see why.

25g/1oz butter
25g/1oz plain flour
1 tsp baking powder
generous pinch of salt
175g/6oz wholemeal flour

25g/1oz medium oatmeal
1 tsp ground cinnamon
2 tbsp chocolate chips
75g/3oz butter
5 tbsp milk

MAKES 14

- Pre-heat the oven to 200°C/400°F/gas mark 6. Lightly butter two non-stick baking trays
- Sift the plain flour, baking powder and salt into a bowl. Add the wholemeal flour, oatmeal, cinnamon and chocolate chips and blend them thoroughly together. Rub in the butter with your fingertips until the mixture resembles breadcrumbs. Add the milk and mix to a firm dough.
- Roll the mixture on a floured work surface into a flat square until it is about 5mm/¼in thick. Cut into squares and place them on the baking trays. Bake in the centre of the oven for 10–12 minutes until they are golden-brown. Allow them to cool and serve with fresh coffee.

Maids of Honour

This recipe is reputed to have been invented for Henry VIII's hand maidens.

25g/1oz butter
150ml/¼pt milk
25g/1oz cake crumbs
50g/2oz butter, cut into small pieces
25g/1oz caster sugar
50g/2oz ground almonds

1 egg, beaten
rind of 1 lemon, grated
almond essence
175g/6oz shortcrust pastry (see page 93)
strawberry jam

MAKES 12

- Pre-heat the oven to 220°C/425°F/gas mark 7. Butter a 12-cake patty tin.
- Gently heat the milk in a saucepan, but do not let it boil, add the cake crumbs, butter, sugar, ground almonds, egg, lemon rind and a few drops of almond essence, stirring all the ingredients together. Leave to stand for 10 minutes.
- Meanwhile, make the pastry, roll it out and cut out 12 rounds using a 7.5cm/3in fluted pastry cutter. Place the pastry into the patty tins and spread a generous layer of strawberry jam over the base of each one. Divide the filling mixture equally into each pastry cup.
- Bake in the centre of the oven for 20 minutes until golden-brown. Allow to cool for 5 minutes before moving from the patty tins.

Pear Sponge

Another Lakeland classic which is dedicated to Rachel, Carol and Michael Fletcher. It is very important to fan the pears out for this recipe as it makes the pattern more attractive and the pears will not break up so easily.

100g/4oz caster sugar
100g/4oz butter
2 eggs
170g/6oz plain flour

½ tsp baking powder
450g/1lb William Pears, peeled, cored and
    thinly sliced (fanned)
2 tbsp caster sugar, for sprinkling

- Pre-heat the oven to 180°C/350°F/gas mark 4.
- In a bowl, place the sugar with the butter and blend together. Add the eggs, blending into a creamy consistency.
- Sift in the flour and baking powder, then fold them into the mixture gently.
- Pour the mixture into a greased and lined flan tin.
- Arrange the pears in small, fan shapes on top of the sponge.
- Bake in the centre of the oven for 1 hour, then while the cake is still hot, sprinkle with the remaining sugar.

Manx Cake

❋

I found this recipe for Rice Cake in my copy of *Warne's Model Cookery* by Mary Jewry, which was published in 1868:

> Half a pound of rice flour; half a pound of white sugar; eight eggs; peel of half a lemon. Well beat eight eggs for half an hour, and stir them into half a pound of rice flour, half a pound of white sugar pounded, and peel of the lemon grated. Mix well together, and bake it in a buttered tin.

❋

I have converted the recipe for the people of the Isle of Man to enjoy.

25g/1oz butter
8 eggs
225g/8oz rice flour

225g/8oz granulated sugar
rind of ½ lemon, grated

• Pre-heat the oven to 190°C/375°F/gas mark 5. Butter a 18cm/7in sandwich cake tin.
• Put the eggs in a blender and blend for 5 minutes or place them into a bowl and use a hand whisk to blend for 10 minutes. Sieve the rice flour into the eggs and blend. Add the sugar and lemon rind and give the mixture a good stir.
• Pour the mixture into the buttered cake tin, cover the top with greased grease-proof paper and bake in the centre of the oven for 40 minutes.

Singing Hinnys

A taste of Tyneside, where 'hinny' is a corruption of honey. The cakes used to be cooked on a gridiron, and they got their name from the 'singing' sound they made as they cooked. In the nineteenth century silver threepenny pieces were inserted in the cakes, which were given to the Geordie children at birthday parties.

350g/12oz self-raising flour
50g/2oz ground rice
pinch of salt
50g/2oz caster sugar

2 tsp baking powder
50g/2oz butter
75g/3oz currants
150ml/¼pt single cream

• Place the flour, ground rice, salt, sugar and baking powder in a mixing bowl and blend together. Add the butter and rub the butter into mixture with your fingertips, until it resembles breadcrumbs, then add the currants and cream to make a soft dough.
• Roll out the dough on a floured surface to about 5mm/½in thick. Shape it into a round and cut into quarters. Bake on a greased griddle (listen to it sing) or in a frying pan for 4 minutes on each side until they are brown. Serve with lashings of butter, jam or clotted cream.

A GREAT BRITISH CHRISTMAS

Lorraine Soup

*Oak-smoked Warwickshire Venison with Beetroot, Apple
and Ginger Chutney and Five Spice Sauce*

Traditional Christmas Pye

Roast Turkey with Orange and Lemon Stuffing

Haunch of Venison with Wild Mushrooms

Salmon and Smoked Trout in Pastry with Herb Sauce

Newhaven Cream with Salmon and Prawns with Parsley Sauce

Crown Roast Loin of Pork with Apple and Chestnut Stuffing

Honey-glazed York Ham with Apricot Compote

Roast Goose with Orange Brandy Sauce

Rich Kent Plum Pudding

Mulled Wine

Christmas Bread and Butter Pudding

Christmas Cake

Don't Drink and Drive Fruit Cup

Red Velvet Beetroot Relish

Grandmother's Homemade Brown Bread

The Victorians and Edwardians delighted in celebrating the festive season. Seeing all their favourite dishes set out on a buffet table must have been an amazing sight, but the extravagant menus were quite normal among middle- and upper-class homes in British homes at Christmas. I still enjoy demonstrating the art of Christmas Past, but because times have changed and we are more informal than ever, the true spirit of Christmas seems to have been forgotten along with the traditional recipes. I thought that you would like to try some Victorian and Edwardian Christmas recipes, which I have converted for today's tastes and more informal lifestyles

Oak-smoked Warwickshire Venison

Lorraine Soup

This soup was named after Mary of Lorraine, mother of Mary, Queen of Scots, who, according to my dear friend Steve Johnstone at Dalhousie Castle, near Edinburgh, introduced the soup while she was visiting Holyrood Palace in Edinburgh. This recipe – for Neville Petts, with thanks – is served at traditional Scottish banquets during the festive season.

25g/1oz butter
25g/1oz flour
1l/1¾pt chicken stock
100g/4oz cooked chicken breast, finely chopped
zest of 1 lemon
¼ nutmeg, freshly grated

150ml/¼pt double cream
25g/1oz crushed almonds
salt and freshly ground white pepper

Garnish
fresh chives and toasted cheese bread

• Place the butter in a saucepan and heat gently. Add the flour and cook for 2 minutes. Slowly add the chicken stock and cook for 12 minutes over a low heat, stirring all the time.
• Add the chicken meat, lemon zest and nutmeg. Cook for a further 12 minutes on a low heat. Stir in the cream, almonds, salt and white pepper, simmer for 4 minutes and serve, garnished with snipped chives and French stick toasted with cheese.

Oak-smoked Warwickshire Venison

WITH BEETROOT, APPLE AND GINGER CHUTNEY AND FIVE SPICE SAUCE

The enjoyable part of writing this book was the opportunity it gave me to tour Britain, and my visit to the Welcombe Hotel and Golf Course, Stratford-on-Avon, Warwickshire, was especially memorable. The head chef, Mark Naylor, supplied me with this wonderful recipe, which is pre-Victorian. Oak-smoked venison can be obtained by mail order from Mike Robbins at the Hart of England Deer Company in Warwick.

4 x 225g/8oz oak-smoked venison steaks

Sauce
300ml/½pt chicken stock
2 tbsp Madeira
¼ tsp five spice powder
25g/1oz unsalted butter
3 tbsp double cream

Chutney
3 shallots, chopped
3 tbsp white wine vinegar
2 bramley apples, peeled, cored and diced
1 bay leaf
4 juniper berries
1 tsp grated ginger
1 tsp soft brown sugar
4 tbsp Red Velvet beetroot, diced

- Make the chutney by gently cooking the chopped shallots in a little of the butter from the sauce ingredients for 3 minutes. Add the vinegar and boil rapidly for 4 minutes. Add the rest of the chutney ingredients except the beetroot and simmer for 6 minutes on a low heat. Remove from the heat, add the beetroot and place into a sauce boat. Keep warm.
- Meanwhile, heat a little butter in a large frying pan, add the steaks and cook gently for 7 minutes each side. Remove the steaks to warm serving plates.
- Add the chicken stock to the pan, bring to the boil for 8 minutes, reducing the chicken stock by half. Add the Madeira and five spice powder and simmer for 2 minutes.
- Add the rest of the butter and double cream and pour around the venison steaks, garnished with the apple and ginger chutney, and deep fried shredded cabbage.

Traditional Christmas Pye

I could not resist this eighteenth-century recipe, which I have converted for the British Christmas. I am sure this would be the highlight of some British tables for although it is quite an expensive dish by today's standards, it is worth every sixpence. The original pie consisted of boned poultry, fitted one inside the other, starting with a turkey, goose, chicken, pigeon and quail, together with sausage meat and hard-boiled eggs in a double thick pastry crust.

50g/2oz butter
1 large onion, finely chopped
175g/6oz button mushrooms
175g/6oz of each of turkey, goose, chicken and York ham, roughly chopped
salt and freshly ground black pepper
6 tbsp brandy

300ml/½ pt turkey stock
1 tsp cornflour blended with a tbsp of port
150ml/¼ pt double cream
350g/12oz shortcrust pastry (see page 93)
175g/6oz sausage meat
4 hard-boiled eggs, shelled
1 egg for washing the pastry

SERVES 8–10

- Pre-heat the oven to 190°C/375°F/gas mark 5.
- In a large saucepan melt the butter, add the onion and mushrooms and cook for 4 minutes. Add the meats and cook for a further 8 minutes. Season well, add the brandy and turkey stock and simmer for 10 minutes. Add the cornflour and double cream and simmer for 2 minutes, remove from the heat and allow to cool.
- Roll out the pastry on a lightly floured surface and use two-thirds to line a 1.5l/2½ pt pie dish. Place the sausage meat in the bottom, cover with the whole hard-boiled eggs and then with the cooled meat mixture.
- Roll out the remaining pastry and cover the pie, pressing gently to seal all round. Brush the pie with beaten egg and decorate with the trimmings. Bake in the centre of the oven for 45–50 minutes.

Roast Turkey

WITH ORANGE AND LEMON STUFFING

John Rae at Piersland House Hotel, Troon, adds a little whisky to his Christmas stuffing to enhance the festive flavour. I know that every one likes turkey at Christmas, but have you ever had turkey with an orange- and lemon-flavoured stuffing? Oven-roasted chestnuts, puréed with a little honey, would combine beautifully with the citrus stuffing.

4.5kg/10lb oven-ready turkey
100g/4oz melted butter
juice of 1 lemon
juice of 1 orange
5 tbsp sweet white wine
2 tbsp mint, freshly chopped

Stuffing
4 tbsp shallots, finely chopped
50g/2oz butter
1 tbsp mint, freshly chopped
450g/1lb Cumberland sausage meat

juice and finely grated rind of 2 lemons and 2
    oranges
100g/4oz fresh brown breadcrumbs
2 tbsp fresh parsley, finely chopped
salt and freshly ground black pepper

Garnish
10 mini pork sausages
10 small slices, rindless streaky bacon
3 oranges and 3 lemons
cranberry jelly
2 sprigs of parsley

SERVES 10

- Pre-heat the oven to 220°C/425°F/gas mark 7.
- First, make the stuffing. Fry the shallots in the butter for 4 minutes, add the mint and cook for 1 minute. Put all the other stuffing ingredients in a large bowl and blend well with the shallots, mint and butter. Stuff the neck end of the turkey, truss the bird and place it on a rack in a large roasting tin.
- Put the butter, orange and lemon juice, wine and mint into a bowl and baste the turkey with the marinade every 20 minutes.
- Place the turkey in the oven and cook for 30 minutes, lower the heat to 180°C/350°F/gas mark 4 and cook for 3 hours. During the last 30 minutes place the sausages and bacon around the turkey.
- Serve with a giblet gravy made from the turkey and basting juices. Garnish with mini pork sausages wrapped in streaky bacon, crowns of orange and lemon filled with cranberry jelly and sprigs of parsley.

Haunch of Venison

WITH WILD MUSHROOMS

Use a cut of venison that has been boned and rolled by the butcher,
and marinade the meat in the mixture for 24 hours before cooking.

1kg/2lb haunch or venison	25g/1oz butter
	2 tbsp olive oil
Marinade	50g/2oz plain flour
1 tbsp chopped ginger	75ml/3fl oz port
4 large onions, chopped	100ml/4fl oz venison marinade (after cooking)
8 cloves	3 tbsp English mustard
300ml/½pt red wine	150ml/¼pt double cream
salt and freshly ground black pepper	175g/6oz wild mushrooms, sliced

SERVES 8

- Pre-heat the oven to 200°C/400°F/gas mark 6.
- Leave the haunch to marinate, then place it in a baking tray with the marinade, cover and bake for 2 hours.
- In a large frying pan heat the butter and oil on a medium heat. Add the flour and cook for 3 minutes. Pour on the port and venison stock and cook for a further 5 minutes. Add the mustard and cream, blending them into the sauce thoroughly. Add the mushrooms, cook for 3 minutes, taste and adjust the seasoning.
- Place the mushroom sauce around the venison and serve with a few roasted chestnuts.
- Save the rest of the marinade for a red wine sauce, which you can make by adding 2 tbsp tomato purée and 12 whole shallots with 100g/4oz cooked rindless bacon, chopped very fine. Place all the ingredients in a saucepan and reduce by half.

Salmon and Smoked Trout
IN PASTRY WITH HERB SAUCE

I make this every year as an alternative to turkey, and it is especially popular with my friends from abroad. The recipe was given to me by an Englishman who, for years, represented the best in British cuisine, Michael Smith. I devised the Herb Sauce for one of the most knowledgeable herb gardeners I know – Steve Wickman at Stephensfield Herbs, Orrell, near Wigan, who grew the herbs so that I could make the sauce. If you have never grown your own herbs, I suggest you really do try. The smell of fresh sage, rosemary and thyme wafting through the house from the garden is heavenly.

2.3kg/5lb salmon, filleted
450g/1lb smoked trout fillet
100g/4oz butter
50g/2oz sultanas
4 tbsp lemon juice
1 tbsp mint, freshly chopped
1 nutmeg, freshly grated
salt and freshly ground black pepper
450g/1lb shortcrust pastry (see page 93)
1 egg, blended with 1 tsp milk

Garnish
sprigs of sage, rosemary and thyme

Sauce
100g/4oz butter
1 onion, finely chopped
2 tbsp parsley, freshly chopped
1 tbsp sage, finely chopped
1 tbsp rosemary, finely chopped
1 tbsp thyme, finely chopped
1 tbsp flour
4 tbsp dry white wine
150ml/1/4pt fish stock
300ml/1/2pt double cream
salt and freshly ground pepper
1 tsp English mustard
2 egg yolks

- Pre-heat the oven to 200°C/400°F/gas mark 6.
- Separate the two salmon fillets. Place the smoked trout on the rough side of one salmon fillet and put the other salmon fillet to one side.
- Melt the butter in a saucepan, add the sultanas, lemon juice, mint, nutmeg, salt and pepper and heat gently. Leave the ingredients to infuse for 10 minutes then spread them over the smoked trout. Place the remaining salmon fillet on top, like a sandwich.
- Roll out the pastry on a floured board, place the salmon on the pastry and wrap the pastry over the salmon, cutting away any surplus pastry. Carefully turn the pastry over onto a greased baking sheet, make scale patterns in the pastry with a fork and brush lightly with the beaten egg. Bake in the centre of the oven for 35 minutes until golden-brown. Remove from the oven and place on a hot serving dish, garnished with sprigs of sage, rosemary and thyme.
- Meanwhile, make the sauce. Melt half the butter in a pan, add the onion and herbs and cook for 4 minutes. Add the flour and cook for 1 minute. Slowly add the wine and fish stock and cook for at least 12 minutes, stirring all the time. Add the cream, salt and pepper, mustard and egg yolks, blend thoroughly, cooking for at least 10 minutes on a low heat, but do not allow the sauce to boil. Remove from the heat and finally add the remaining butter, cut into pieces, and serve in a sauce boat with the Salmon and Smoked Trout.

Newhaven Cream
WITH SALMON AND PRAWNS WITH PARSLEY SAUCE

This steamed fish pudding comes from the fishing village of Newhaven on the outskirts of Edinburgh. It makes an excellent alternative Christmas starter or fish course. Finnan haddock is used with the recipe, but because it is a Christmas treat, I have added some fresh salmon and prawns.

450g/1lb smoked finnan haddock fillet, skin and bones removed
450g/1lb salmon fillet, skin and bones removed
450g/1lb fresh uncooked prawns
1l/1¾pt fresh milk
100g/4oz butter
250g/10oz fresh white breadcrumbs
3 tbsp sherry
¼ tsp nutmeg

4 tbsp fresh parsley, chopped
10 fresh eggs
salt and freshly ground black pepper

Sauce
25g/1oz butter
25g/1oz plain flour
milk from the fish
4 tbsp double cream
1 tbsp parsley, freshly chopped

SERVES 8

• Pre-heat the oven to 200°C/400°F/gas mark 6.
• Place the fish in a large saucepan and cover with the milk. Bring slowly to the boil, cover the saucepan and simmer gently for 15 minutes. Using a slotted spoon, carefully remove the fish and prawns to a large mixing bowl, reserving the milk to make the sauce.
• Add the remaining ingredients to the fish and blend thoroughly, season well with a little salt and freshly ground black pepper.
• Grease a large ovenproof deep casserole and pour in the mixture, cover with greaseproof paper and secure with string. Place in a large baking tray, half filled with water, and cook in the oven for 80 minutes until set.
• Meanwhile, make the sauce. Melt the butter in a saucepan, add the flour and the milk from the fish, cook for 5 minutes, stirring all the time, add the cream and parsley, season to taste and pour into a sauce-boat and serve with the Newhaven Cream.

Crown Roast Loin of Pork

WITH APPLE AND CHESTNUT STUFFING

A crown roast always looks spectacular and is an ideal dish for the festive season.
Ask your butcher to prepare the crown for you. Otherwise follow my instructions,
it is simple and straightforward.

1–2 loins of pork with 10–12 cutlets, chined
salt and freshly ground black pepper
2 tbsp corn oil
1 large onion, chopped
2 large cooking apples, peeled, cored and
  chopped

4 tbsp chestnut purée
225g/8oz Cumberland sausage meat
75g/3oz fresh white breadcrumbs
1 egg
1 tsp sage

SERVES 8

• Heat the oven to 180°C/350°F/gas mark 4.
• Trim each cutlet bone to a depth of 2.5cm/1in, trim off any excess fat and season well with salt and freshly ground black pepper. Bend the joints around, fat side inwards, and sew the crown together using butcher's string or strong cotton. Completely cover the exposed bones with buttered tin foil.
• Prepare the stuffing. Heat the oil in a large saucepan, add the onion and fry gently for 3 minutes. Remove the pan from the heat and add the remaining ingredients, blending them thoroughly with a wooden spoon.
• Place the crown of pork on a baking tray and fill the centre of the crown with the stuffing. Bake in the centre of the oven for 90–100 minutes Remove the foil from the bones and serve with baked parsnips and roast potatoes.

Honey-glazed York Ham
WITH APRICOT COMPOTE

York ham was served to Queen Victoria with this famous compote every Christmas.
She was also fond of cloves, so should you wish to stud the ham with cloves during the baking
process, do so. Scotts of York have been curers of Yorkshire hams and bacon for centuries.

2kg/4lb York ham
1 onion stuck with 6 cloves
1 bay leaf
8 peppercorns
300ml/½pt sweet white wine
50g/2oz soft brown sugar

175ml/6fl oz crushed or puréed apricots and
  juice
2 tbsp clear honey, warmed

Garnish
275g/10oz apricots, sliced

SERVES 8–10

- Pre-heat the oven to 200°C/400°F/gas mark 6.
- Soak the ham in sufficient cold water to cover for 4 hours, then discard the
water. Put the ham in a large saucepan with the onion, bay leaf, peppercorns and
the white wine. Add just sufficient cold water to cover. Bring to the boil, cover the
pan and simmer gently for 2 hours.
- Place the brown sugar, apricot purée and juice and warmed honey into a bowl
and mix together.
- Drain the ham, strain the stock and use it in homemade soup.
- Remove the skin from the ham, and score the fat into a diamond pattern across the
face of the ham. Place the ham in a baking tray and completely smother with the apricot
compote mixture. Bake in the centre of the oven for 1 hour, basting every 15 minutes.
- Place the ham on a serving dish, garnished with sliced apricots and the juices
from the roasting tin.

Roast Goose

WITH ORANGE BRANDY SAUCE

The breast on a goose should be plump and the skin should be white. Stuff the goose with your favourite stuffing and chopped apples, then place it on a wire rack in a roasting tray so that the fat can drain away from the goose as it cooks. Allow 20 minutes per pound of meat, with an extra 20 minutes' cooking time at the end.

5–6kg/10–12lb Norfolk goose
50g/2oz butter
2 tbsp olive oil
150ml/¼pt orange brandy
25g/1oz plain flour
150ml/¼pt fresh orange juice
50g/2oz courgettes, cut into very fine strips
50g/2oz red peppers, cut into very fine strips
50g/2oz leeks, shredded

salt and freshly ground black pepper
3 fresh oranges, cut into segments and the
    rind cut into very fine strips
2 tbsp fresh tarragon, chopped
150ml/¼pt fromage frais

Garnish
fresh tarragon leaves
strips of orange rind

SERVES 10

- Pre-heat the oven to 200°C/400°F/gas mark 6 and roast the goose in the centre of the oven for 60 minutes. Baste with the goose fat, reduce the oven temperature to 180°C/350°F/gas mark 4 and cook for a further 2 hours.
- Heat the butter and oil in a large frying pan add the orange brandy and cook for 2 minutes, sprinkle lightly with the flour and cook for a further minute. Reduce the heat and add the orange juice, courgettes, peppers and leeks, season with salt and freshly ground black pepper and simmer for 4 minutes until the sauce is reduced and thickens.
- Add half the orange segments, the rind, tarragon and fromage frais and cook for a further 2 minutes.
- Thinly slice the goose meat and arrange the meat in a fan shape on the stuffing, around the centre of a large warm plate, with a little sauce. Garnish with segments of orange and fresh tarragon leaves and sprinkle the goose meat with fresh strips of orange rind.

Rich Kent Plum Pudding

This rich, dark pudding was originally known as Sussex or Lent Pudding, and it was copied, with different names, all over the country. In the Midlands, for example, it was known as Feast Plum Pudding, and Deddington had a Pudden Pie, which was made for the fairs that travelled around the country in the eighteenth and early nineteenth centuries.

25g/1oz butter
100g/4oz cooking apple, diced
200g/7oz dried figs, chopped
100g/4oz currants
100g/4oz sultanas
225g/8oz raisins
200g/7oz blanched almonds, chopped
25g/1oz hazelnuts, chopped
100g/4oz Brazil nuts, chopped

175g/6oz stale white breadcrumbs
1 tsp mixed spice
100g/4oz soft brown sugar
100g/4oz cut mixed peel
1 lemon, juice and rind
100g/4oz softened butter
100g/4oz clear honey, warmed
3 eggs, beaten with 2 tbsp dark rum
6 tbsp brandy

SERVES 8–10

• Butter two 750ml/1¼pt pudding basins. Prepare a double-steamer or two large saucepans to hold the pudding basins. You need to be able to fill them at least three-quarters full with water.

• Put the fruit, dried fruits, nuts, breadcrumbs, spice, sugar, peel, lemon juice and rind in a large mixing bowl.

• In a saucepan melt the softened butter and honey together on a very low heat, allow to cool slightly and gently beat in the eggs and rum. Pour the liquid over the dried ingredients, stirring thoroughly. Give a final stir and add half the brandy.

• Spoon the mixture into the greased basins, cover with greased greaseproof paper and secure with string.

• Place the basins into the steamer or pans, slowly bring the water to the boil, cover and lower the heat and simmer for 3 hours, topping up with hot water when required.

• Allow the pudding to settle for at least 4 hours, then steam again for a further hour before serving.

• Put 3 tbsp of brandy in a metal soup ladle and heat over a low flame, ignite and pour over the pudding when serving, garnished with a sprig of holly.

Mulled Wine

It is easy to say do not use cheap wine for this recipe, but for a really unique flavour please do not use any old plonk and do not allow the mull to boil at any stage of cooking.

225g/8oz caster sugar
300ml/½pt water
2 bottles red wine

1 bottle port
1 lemon stuck with 8 cloves
1 small cinnamon stick

SERVES 12

• Put the sugar and water in a large saucepan and heat gently to dissolve the sugar. Add the wine, port, lemon stuck with cloves and cinnamon stick , re-heat gently until the mulled wine is just hot, cover and leave for 15 minutes.

• Remove the cinnamon stick and heat gently again but do not boil. Pour into a punch bowl with the lemon stuck with cloves.

Christmas Bread and Butter Pudding

Every Christmas is the same – there is always lots of bread left over and jars of mince-meat, bottles and bottles of milk and butter coming out of our ears. So, what better way to use them all up, than to make a Christmas Bread and Butter Pudding.

25g/1oz butter	3 eggs
12 slices of bread and butter	50g/2oz soft brown sugar
50g/2oz sultanas	
400g/14oz or 1 jar of mincemeat, warmed	grated nutmeg
1 tsp nutmeg, freshly ground	brown sugar
600ml/1pt milk	

SERVES 8

• Pre-heat the oven to 180°C/350°F/gas mark 4. Grease a 2l/3½ pt baking dish with 25g/1oz butter.
• Cut the bread into triangles and arrange in layers, buttered side up and sprinkled with sultanas, spreading over the mincemeat and grated nutmeg and finishing with a top layer of bread, arranged in a neat pattern.
• Heat the milk in a saucepan, but do not let it boil. Beat the eggs in a bowl with the sugar and whisk in the hot milk. Strain the custard mixture over the bread, finish with a little more grated nutmeg and a little more brown sugar.
• Leave the dish to stand for 45 minutes, then bake in the centre of the oven for 35–40 minutes until the custard is set.

Christmas Cake

This is also my recipe for wedding cake, and when it is kept in an airtight tin, double wrapped in greaseproof paper and cooking foil, it will keep for up to six months. Until the middle of the nineteenth century, Christmas Cake – Plum Cake – was served plain, not iced.

225g/8oz butter	6 eggs, whisked
225g/8oz caster sugar	450g/1lb currants
drops of gravy browning	225g/8oz raisins
225g/8oz plain flour, sifted with ¼ tsp baking powder	100g/4oz glacé cherries, chopped
	50g/2oz peel, chopped
pinch of salt	100g/4oz blanched, chopped almonds
1 tsp mixed spice	4 tbsp of rum

SERVES 10–12

• Pre-heat the oven to 160°C/325°F/gas mark 3. Line a 25cm/10in cake tin with greaseproof paper.

- Place the butter and sugar in a very large bowl and stir until completely blended. Add a few drops of gravy browning.
- Sift the flour with the baking powder, salt and mixed spice. Add the flour and the egg mixture alternately and very carefully to the butter and sugar until both ingredients are used up.
- Add the remaining ingredients and stir until everything is completely blended.
- Let the mixture settle for 1 hour and give it a final stirring. Put the mixture into the cake tin, and cover the top with a piece of greaseproof paper. Bake in the centre of the oven for 45 minutes. Lower the heat to 140°C/275°F/gas mark 1 for 4 hours.
- Remove the cake and allow the cake to cool completely before you remove it from the tin. Remove the paper. Turn the cake over and sprinkle the bottom with 4 tbsp of brandy.
- Double wrap the cake in greaseproof paper, then in cooking foil. Place the cake into a large biscuit tin and store in a cool place for at least a week before decorating and icing for Christmas.

Don't Drink and Drive Fruit Cup

This is not only a life-saver but also a job-saver for those of us who have a long drive ahead of us after the festive non-alcoholic fun, this really is a refreshing drink with a kick!

2 lemons
2 oranges
1.2l/2pt ice cold water

300ml/½pt concentrated Vimto drink
600ml/1pt ginger beer
2 cloves

SERVES 15

- Slice the lemons and oranges, place them into a large jug or punch bowl, add the water and Vimto and chill for 2 hours.
- Add the ginger beer and cloves and chill again for 15 minutes before serving.

Red Velvet Beetroot Relish

The finest beetroots in Britain come from the north of England, and the area around Scarisbrick and Southport is known as Red Velvet country, for hundreds of acres of this very special beetroot grow there. Serve this relish with chunks of your favourite cheese and my Grandmother's Homemade Brown Bread and butter.

■ 139 ■

900g/2lb Red Velvet cooked beetroot, diced
450g/1lb white cabbage, finely shredded
1 large onion, finely shredded
75g/3oz fresh horseradish, finely grated
1 tsp English mustard powder

600ml/1pt red wine vinegar
225g/8oz brown sugar
100g/4oz sultanas
pinch of grated nutmeg
salt and freshly ground black pepper

MAKES 900G/2LB

- Place all the ingredients in a large saucepan, bring the pan to the boil slowly and allow the ingredients to infuse for 30 minutes. Return the saucepan to the heat and simmer gently for 30 minutes.
- Spoon the beetroot relish into clean, warm jars, cover and seal with vinegar-proof tops. Store in a cool, dry, dark place and leave to mature for 6 weeks.

Grandmother's Homemade Brown Bread

I remember my grandmother making this traditional Lancashire loaf when I was a child.

450g/1lb wholemeal or Hovis flour
1 tsp salt
7g/¼oz lard, softened
1 tsp soft brown sugar

300ml/½pt warm milk
15g/½oz fresh yeast
1 tbsp warm honey
wholemeal flour and poppy seed for sprinkling

- Pre-heat the oven to 230°C/450°F/gas mark 8. Lightly grease a loaf tin.
- Place the wholemeal flour and salt in a bowl, gently rub in the lard and make a well in the centre.
- Add the sugar to the warm milk and whisk until dissolved, then use 2 tbsp to blend the yeast into a paste. Add the rest of the milk to the yeast and pour into the well.
- Blend the mixture thoroughly, knead the dough for 10 minutes, then shape it into a ball and place it in a buttered bowl. Cover with kitchen film and put in a warm place to rise for 60 minutes. Dust your work surface with wholemeal flour and knead the dough for 2 minutes to work out the air.
- Place the dough in the loaf tin, cover with kitchen film and put in a warm place for 30 minutes. Remove the film, put in the centre of the oven and bake for 30 minutes.
- Brush the top lightly with honey, sprinkle with the wholemeal flour and poppy seeds and return to the oven for a further 10 minutes.

Acknowledgements

I shall look back on the two years I spent working on this book with happiness and pride. Happiness because it has been a thoroughly enjoyable experience, and pride because I was able to meet numerous people whose knowledge and understanding of British food are second to none. It was a privilege for me to talk to these enthusiasts who are involved in the British food industry every day of their lives and who put their hearts and souls into promoting and encouraging us to buy and cook with the finest produce in the world.

I would like to thank all the following, who agree with me that we produce some of the finest food and have some of the best recipes in the world, and that we can hold our heads high in any country and any continent in the world: the Olverson family, who gave Britain Red Velvet beetroot, the most underrated of vegetables, especially Brian for all his help and advice, and Sue and Peter Vickers for introducing me to Red Velvet; David George, the best photographer I know and ever-lasting friend, with whom I spent the long days and nights photographing Britain; and truly British Nicholas Lander, who kindly wrote the Foreword.

We are a herb-loving society, and without herbs our food would be tasteless and bland, so it is to Steve Wickman and Suzanne and Julie at Stephensfield Herbs, Orrell, near Wigan, that I say an extremely large thank you for supplying my kitchen and herb garden with the Stephensfield products over the last year.

Thanks also to: quality butcher Robert Anderson, whose shop in Rosewell, Midlothian, really is special; Jurg and Jane Bleiker of Bleikers Smoke House, Harrogate; Geoffrey John, the chairman, and Mike Callaghan of Food from Britain; Low Laithe Trout Farm; Mike Hollins of Hart of England Deer Farm, Warwickshire; McCartney's family butchers and their award-winning sausages of Main Street, Moira, County Down, Northern Ireland; Sue Webb, McNeills Fine Food and Rose Industries at Rotherfield Greys, Henley-on-Thames; Brian Kilkenny and Derek Andrews at the Meat and Livestock Commission; Robin Scott at Nidderdale Trout Farm, Harrogate; Arthur Cunynghame, the only person who can talk cheese 24 hours a day, and everyone at Paxton & Whitfield, Stratford-on-Avon, for setting up the selection of British cheeses; Stephen Bailey of G. Scott, York; and Martin Holmes at Sea Breeze, Pepper Street, Nantwich, for the fishy stories.

Many thanks also to the following people and their hotels and restaurants for letting David George and myself stay at their establishments during our tour of Britain: everyone at Bentley's Seafood Restaurant and Oyster Bar, London; Julian Groom at the Cavendish Hotel, Jermyn Street, London, and Tommy Langley, Mayfair's celebrated barman, who is renowned for his British cocktails at the Cavendish; Barry Rea, Coppull Moor, Chorley, Lancashire, whose advice is always refreshing and very much appreciated; Neville Petts and

Mutton pies from Robert Anderson's shop in Rosewell near Troon

Steve Johnstone at Dalhousie Castle, the finest hotel in Edinburgh; Diane and Gordon Whyte at Edenvale House, Newtownards, Northern Ireland; Ann and Pat Gallagher of Gallaghers, Little Scotland, Blackrod, Lancashire; Jane and Andrew Cousar at the Glenside Hotel, Troon, for the British Breakfast of the Year; Geoffrey Tucker, David Hinds and Jeremy Stone at my favourite Welsh hotel, Llyndir Hall at Rossett, near Chester; Michael and Carol Fletcher and everyone at the Nanny Brow Country House Hotel in the Lake District; John Rae, the head chef and Michael Lee, the general manager, at Piersland House Hotel, Troon; Pamela Henderson, Antoinette Freeman-Danby and Johnathon Brown, Redworth Hall Hotel and Country Club; Jeremy Rata ('The Golden Oldie'), Dave Alton and his talented sous chef, Dave Edwards, at Rookery Hall, Nantwich; Jon Moore and Mark Naylor at the Welcombe Hotel and Golf Course, Stratford-on-Avon; Euan Rodger and Andrew Jones, the Worsley Arms, Hovingham, Yorkshire; Barry Aspinall and his team at Wrightington Country Club and Blazers restaurant near Standish, Wigan, Lancashire; Gerrard and Ruth Booth (they say they are my Number One fans), Hubert and Carol Lowery for their love and wonderful advice on Northern Ireland; my dear friend Tom Rowntree, who is now with the Green Park Hotel, Half Moon Street, London, who introduced me to several establishments; and Beth Coyne. Finally, my wife Jayne – without her, I would be nothing.

If I have forgotten anyone, it was not intentional ... thank you all ... and enjoy.

Index